The Truth about addiction according to God's Word

A message from the Author,...

Dear reader,...

This book that you're holding in your hands contains the power and wisdom of God's Truth that can change and save the lives of millions of otherwise lost souls who are dying from addictions to drugs, alcohol, and other sin.

God's Word, The Truth tells us that if we're SAVED, we should be SOBER. On the other hand, False teachings, and or the misunderstanding of scripture such as 1 John 1:8-10, or Romans 7:14-20, has deceived millions of people into believing that "No, we're all just innocent sinners." Whenever someone tries to correct or rebuke someone for any of their sinful behavior, their first reaction in defense of themselves is, "we're all sinners," based on the message in 1 John 1:8-10, which was **not** written as a license, or permission to sin! It is a message to teach us that when we are weak and overtaken by the many temptations of satan, and unwillingly fall into sin, if we mournfully admit it, with a broken heart, repent of it, and faithfully turn back to God, He will forgive us. Until we learn to understand this simple Truth, we will continue to willfully sin, because we've believed a lie that it's ok to sin if we "just believe in God." Rarely, if ever have we been taught Acts 26:20, to Repent, and show it by our actions! Or to simply examine 1 John, chapter 2 for an explanation. If we're alcoholics and addicts, and have been led to believe that Christ's shed Blood on The Cross is an excuse to sin, Recovery and Eternal Life with Him is probably not in our future. To be SAVED and SOBER, we must Repent,…have the Faith of a mustard seed,…be obedient to His Word and will for us,…and confess that Jesus is Lord!

This book was written for anyone living under the curse of addictions to alcohol, drugs, pornography, gambling, etc. And for their families, loved ones, friends, employers, pastors, counselors, and mentors who counsel according to God's Word and Truth. Or, if you're a Christian who feels led to serve in a ministry to disciple those in your church or neighborhood who may be suffering from addictions, this book contains the information that you need to know to help counsel and mentor them, and share with them Gods Word as it applies to their addictions. **GOD** has no desire for His children to suffer in the bondage of addictions. Galatians 5:1, "Stand fast therefore in the liberty wherewith Christ hath made us free, and be not entangled again with the yoke of bondage." Romans 8:21, "that the creation itself will be liberated from its bondage to decay and brought into the freedom and glory of the children of God." God wants His children to accept Christ as their Savior, and to be "set free from the bondage of addictions." (John 8: 32) This book is dedicated to teach these and other basic Truths through God's Word, to anyone struggling with addictions. Truths that will lead those who follow them to be **SAVED and SOBER!**

This book contains a wealth of scripture used to validate God's Truth relating to addiction recovery, and is quoted in several translations. C.S. Lewis told us we should teach, share, and spread the Gospel Truth of Christ in the vernacular, the language of those who we're trying to reach, so that they may understand God's Truth. In keeping with the very real fact that most people who are struggling to stay clean and sober, are also struggling to make sense of reality, I've tried to keep this book simple and easy to understand. Since the Bible can be difficult for many people to understand and is printed in a variety of translations, some of which seem to contradict others, I've trusted The Holy Spirit to lead me to choose the clearest version of a passage, without losing its meaning, or the Truth.

SAVED and SOBER

DON JOHNSON

Published by
Don Johnson

Copyright © 2012 by Don Johnson
All rights reserved.

ISBN-13: 978-1482594317

ACKNOWLEDGMENTS

This Book is dedicated to the many hundreds of men and women I've had the opportunity to know over the past 30 years struggling with addiction recovery, both in and out of Christian churches. Beginning in AA clubs and meeting rooms, long before churches ever gave thought to supporting a hopeless alcoholic or an addict. And more recently in today's Churches, including many modern mega Churches with a host of programs for the millions of Christians lost in addictions to drugs, alcohol, and other sin. May each of you find Eternal hope in your recovery through God's Love, Grace, and Truth, as shared throughout the pages of this book.

I would like to share my sincerest gratitude to all my brothers and sisters in Christ, who have influenced my Faith and encouraged me over the years, as I trudged along in my own journey of recovery.

A special heartfelt "Thank You" to Pastor Lyn Sahr, who led me to Christ almost 28 years ago to the day! Had God not led him to plant the seed, this book would still be a tree! And I would probably be dead and rotting in hell! His initial guidance has kept me on the right path in spite of the many times I've drifted down dead-end roads, along my journey. His wisdom has kept me focused on The Cross of Christ and His Gospel Truth.

And finally to my family, whose infinite patience has prevailed. To my Mother whose decades of prayers and endless Faith will result in us being reunited someday at "home," with our Father in Heaven. And a special token of appreciation, gratitude, and Love to my beautiful daughter Sarah, whose life has been an unfathomable blessing and inspiration to me! The second brightest light in my life. God being the First!

INTRODUCTION

"Our God is an awesome God; He reigns from Heaven above, with wisdom, power, and love, our God is an awesome God!" ***Anyone*** addicted to alcohol, drugs, or any other sin, needs an Awesome God who reigns from Heaven above, with wisdom, power, Love, ***and,*** Amazing Grace! To save wretches like us, to break the chains of bondage and set us free from our addictions! Only by His Infinite Love and His Amazing Grace is this possible! We need every bit of His Wisdom, Power, Love, and Grace we can get, every minute of every day. The ***only*** way to accomplish this is through our total surrender, commitment, and obedience to God, and His Son Jesus Christ, through the power of the Holy Spirit! All other means and methods of addiction recovery are temporary at best.

Addiction to drugs and alcohol has become an out of control epidemic in this country and around the world. If you're trapped in this epidemic, either directly or indirectly, you need to read this book. If you're not already Born Again and Saved, please take a moment now, before reading any further, to pray and admit to God that you're a sinner, as we all are, ask God to forgive you, and to come into, and take over your life, and to free you from the pain and despair of this sinful life and its addictions. These addictions, whatever they are, that have led you to picking up this book. Promise Him that you'll repent, and turn from your sin, and surrender to Him. In return, He promises you forgiveness and Eternal Life with Him and to "Set You Free" from your addictions! It may take awhile, according to His timing, but as you study His Word, have Fellowship with Him and other believers, develop your Faith and a close personal relationship with Him, you'll begin to recognize that His Word is the Truth, and the world's lies no longer apply to you.

You'll discover that you can be "Set free," (John 8:31-36) and celebrate Victory over your bondage to addictions! (1 John 5:4) This promise is Gods Truth! You'll become a brand new person! (2 Cor. 5:17) And you will be **"SAVED** and **SOBER"**! For evermore! Amen! This is an important step to take before reading this book in order for it to make any sense to you, you must be Born Again. (John 3:3)

This book is filled with God's Word and scripture, and He tells us that His Word is "foolishness" to those who are not His! (1 Corinthians 1:18), "For the preaching of the cross is to them that perish foolishness; but unto us which are saved it is the power of God." It's been written using Gods Word, the Truth, to point those who are struggling with addictions, as well as anyone engaged in trying to help them, in the right direction. To the only *real* answer, which the world has been avoiding for decades. To God! To the one and only true God, who sacrificed His Son, Jesus Christ, on the Cross for our freedom and eternal life! I've referenced thousands of verses of scripture throughout this book, wherever possible, so that readers might follow along and participate as the Bereans did in Acts 17:11, "Now the Bereans were of more noble character than the Thessalonians, for they received the message with great eagerness and examined the Scriptures every day to see if what Paul said was true."

Drug, alcohol, and other destructive addictions are destroying the world around us, one family at a time. One father, mother, child, grandchild, or grandparent at a time. Usually, and consequently, affecting, if not destroying the entire family structure! It's become such a misunderstood and wrongly diagnosed epidemic that our governments and social services, as well as the various professional care givers, (doctors, therapists, counselors, etc., the many various 12-step addiction recovery programs, group homes and treatment facilities), and unfortunately, even most of our Churches, are all at a loss for an answer. Although they all ***proclaim*** to have all the answers and great success rates, the proof is in the pudding! The success rate is minimal, and the relapse rate is out of control! While no one will admit it, all one has to do to see the truth, is look around them to see our entire society spiraling out of control into moral decay. With homelessness, an overloaded welfare system, overcrowded prisons and jails, suicides and heroin overdoses now on the rise in our high schools, an epidemic of serious DUI accidents, and hit-n-runs, often resulting in fatalities, and often by drunk drivers with multiple DUI convictions, anyone who suggests we *don't* have a massive, out of control problem, or that the many different current programs *are* working, has their head in the sand, and is in total denial of reality! At best!

    The general public's naivety regarding addiction recovery, would suggest great success in spite of the obvious increase of this addiction epidemic, however fails to recognize or admit that many of their perceived "success" stories are only valid until that individual fails. They don't admit, or fail to understand that most of their "clients" who relapse or fail, after a year or two or more, out of embarrassment, rarely will come back and admit their failure. Human nature and pride keeps them in fear of the truth. A form of denial and sense of complete failure keeps them from returning to a program, and admitting their failure. They've been mislead into believing that as long as they keep attending these meetings they'll be fine. One of the 12-step clichés is, "keep coming back, it works!" If a program worked, there would be no reason to "keep coming back," or continuing in it. If you go to school to learn a trade, once you've learned it, you don't stay in school; you get a job and practice that trade. Of course it works for some, for a period of time depending on the effort they put into it, or until it *"doesn't" work any longer,* then members are so embarrassed, they stop going back. Take for example, even at the level of your local neighborhood 12-step meeting facility, Mr. Doe attends meetings regularly for a year or two, enthusiastically sharing his great success and giving all the credit to the program and "some *undefined* higher power", whatever that might be. Mr. Doe goes into the programs record books as a success story. Then suddenly one day, Mr. Doe quits coming to the meetings and drops out of sight. Since these meetings are "anonymous", few if anyone really know Mr. Doe, or where he is, or what might have happened to him. More than likely the answer is always going to be that Mr. Doe slipped and failed in his sobriety, and is too embarrassed to face those he had been bragging to about his success. And likewise, the program is not going to list Mr. Doe as a failure for the same reason. Pride over Truth! It exists everywhere today, including in addiction recovery meetings. It's one of the leading reasons for the failure of today's recovery programs efforts to control what has become an epidemic, or plague.

    Another example to consider might be the fact that addiction recovery has become a billion dollar a year industry, with new treatment facilities and group homes popping up every day on every other street corner like banks and convenience stores. 12-step meetings have now evolved into $1000 dollar-a-day treatment facilities with names like, "The Golden Sunset Residential Treatment Center by the Beach," complete with butler and maid service, and maybe a little ***champagne***? It's become a very profitable business, which bleeds corporate America, insurance companies, some Government services (tax payers), and wealthy Americans out of billions of dollars every year. Do you think these "for profit" business's are going to admit to the responsibility of any failures? Absolutely not, and to the contrary, they report and advertise, fraudulently, only the success stories. When a client fails, (relapses), if that client should happen to be a famous sports or entertainment celebrity or politician, or famous socialite, and the story makes the news, the news media can't report that so-and-so just finished a program at a certain facility for liability reasons. So the general public is kept pretty much in the dark about the reality of the facts and numbers that show that these programs rarely work. Thousands of famous celebrity's careers have been destroyed, and millions of common, everyday working class, innocent lives have been destroyed because of addictions to drugs and alcohol.

And the thousands of secular recovery programs and treatment facilities take or accept no responsibility, by hiding their "failure" rates, and saying, "we've done all we can do," or, "they must not have been working the steps!" I've heard this last comment a million times in reference to someone who has relapsed! If common sense prevailed, it should be perfectly clear that these constant news stories of celebrities failing over and over again until they O.D. or just drop out of sight, is evidence that today's typical addiction recovery programs don't work. And again if common sense prevailed, it should also be perfectly clear that these constant news stories of celebrities failing over and over again until they O.D. or just drop out of sight, never mention the millions of common, everyday working class, innocent lives that have been destroyed because of addictions to drugs and alcohol, is evidence that today's typical addiction recovery programs don't work. They only prolong the pain and suffering until the victims do drop out of sight or OD and or die! The above examples are why true relapse statistics are unknown or unreliable today, because many of those who relapse, especially over and over again, eventually drop out of sight! They're either in hospitals, mental institutions, homeless, in jails or prisons, or ***dead!***

Another unknown statistic of the consequences of addictions, are the trickle-down affects on society and the general public. Every aspect and element of our society is affected in some way, either directly or indirectly. For example, how much of the federal, state, or local budgets are impacted by addictions? In Colorado, the state, county, and local budgets for the judicial system, the prisons, jails, and the staff to run them, have quadrupled in the past few decades. The healthcare and welfare budgets cannot be far behind, as well as all the other hidden costs related to this pandemic. In Denver, the fire department and emergency medical responders answer 100's of calls a day for drug and alcohol related emergencies. This alone amounts to millions of dollars a year in taxpayers money. How much of our current recession can be attributed, at least indirectly to the trickle-down consequences of this addiction crisis? The list goes on and on, and on.

Without question, the moral decline of the world in which we ***all*** reside, and are affected by, is both directly and indirectly attributed to the widespread epidemic of drug and alcohol abuse over the past 50 years or more. When I was a child growing up 60 years ago, pornography was considered a picture of a girl in a bathing suit, then a bikini, and then her underwear! Look how far our "civilized" planet has progressed! Pornography has now become "uncivilized" pollution referred to as "adult entertainment", available in our homes on the internet 24/7, and is quickly spreading into public television! And now "child porn" seems to be the #1 box office hit!

This sewer just keeps getting deeper, and no-one can get their head out of the sand long enough to do anything about it! Our Governments are so "asleep at the wheel," they spend all their time, and **our** resources regulating "air pollution," while this "air-wave" internet "pollution" goes unregulated, unchecked, and un-enforced! All because the purveyors of this garbage demand their first amendment rights. We should free all the inhabitants of our zoos, and replace them with the human race! Or maybe just the politicians who are "asleep at the wheel," and failing to do their jobs and make laws to protect us! And, **Yes,** absolutely without a doubt, drug and alcohol abuse, gone completely unchecked over the past 50 or more years, has led us to this state of immoral decline where we find ourselves today! Like cancer, when you ignore it, **or,** out of denial, you call it a common cold, it will only continue to grow until it kills you!

For those who were attracted to this book by its cover, hopefully you already understand the reason for this dilemma our planet finds itself stuck in today. For those who don't know, it's really quite simple! It all boils down to this one simple Truth. For those of us who believe in Gods Truth, and understand its basic fundamental message, the fact is that we have an adversary, Satan. The master of deceit, death, and destruction. Satan has many ways of destroying us and keeping us from Eternal Life with God. This epidemic of drug and alcohol addiction, and the subsequent moral decay of society, and the veil of deception it's been hidden in by Satan, may very well be his most effective, destructive, and deadliest weapon of all to destroy us. His lies and deceitfulness have been keeping the world in darkness since the beginning of time, in the garden, and are still doing so today. Man's inability to recognize, understand, or believe and trust in Gods Truth, have kept Satan in the driver's seat of addictions, and guided the *worlds* secular methods of addiction recovery, to lead millions of lost souls to their death and destruction in hell!

God's Word, The Truth tells us that *if* we're **SAVED**, we should be **SOBER**. On the other hand, False teachings, and or the misunderstanding of scripture such as 1 John 1:8-10, or Romans 7:14-20, has deceived millions of people into believing that "No, we're all just innocent sinners." Whenever someone tries to correct or rebuke any of our sinful behavior, our first reaction in defense of ourselves is, "we're all sinners." Based on the message in 1 John 1:8-10, which was not written as a license or permission to sin! It is a message to teach us that when we are weak and overtaken by the temptations of satan, and unwillingly fall into sin, if we mournfully admit it, with a broken heart repent of it, and faithfully turn back to God, He will forgive us. Until we learn to understand this simple Truth, we will continue to willfully sin, because we've believed a lie that it's ok to sin if we "just believe in God." Rarely, if ever have we been taught Acts 26:20, to Repent, and show it by our actions! Or to simply examine 1 John, chapter 2 for an explanation. If we're alcoholics and addicts, and have been led to believe that Christ's shed Blood on The Cross is an excuse to sin, Recovery and Eternal Life with Him is probably not in our future. To be **SAVED** and **SOBER,** we must Repent,…have the Faith of a mustard seed,…be obedient to His Word and will for us,…and confess that Jesus is Lord!

The purpose of this book is to expose the many lies Satan and his followers have been using for decades, to mislead millions of people struggling with addictions, from finding the Truth, which will lead them to victory and Eternal Recovery. One Step, John 3:3, "Be Born Again," through Faith, will "Set you Free" and give you the "Power", to never want to use drugs or alcohol again! It will still be your choice, but if you read this book, you'll be equipped with the facts based on God's Word and Truth to help you make the *right* choice. You'll be **SAVED AND SOBER!** May God Bless you through this journey of discovery.

CONTENTS

A MESSAGE FROM THE AUTHOR..........................1
ACKNOWLEDGEMENTS..5
INTRODUCTION..6
CHAPTER 1   ADDICTION:
LIFE ON THE BATTLEGROUND...............................16
CHAPTER 2   THE MANY BATTLEGROUNDS
OF ADDICTIONS..24
CHAPTER 3   THE MANY WEAPONS OF
THE ENEMY..30
CHAPTER 4   BE BORN AGAIN..............................45
CHAPTER 5   BE SET FREE.................................... 55
CHAPTER 6   SET FREE FROM HABITUAL SIN........ 65
CHAPTER 7   TRUTH OR CONSEQUENCES............72
CHAPTER 8   DENIAL.. 84
CHAPTER 9   ENABLING.. 96
CHAPTER 10 MENTORING 106
CHAPTER 11 BROKEN HEARTS
AND FAMILIES 124
CHAPTER 12 CHILD ABANDONMENT
AND ABUSE 132
CHAPTER 13 A BIBLE STUDY FOR
ADDICTION RECOVERY...................................... 146
CHAPTER 14 ARE YOU READY
FOR CHANGE?.. 152
CHAPTER 15 CONCLUSION................................. 162

CHAPTER 1

Addiction: Life on the Battleground

Psalm 18:39, NIV,
*"You armed me with strength for **battle;** you made my adversaries bow at my feet."*

Soon after World War 2 ended, World War 3 began! And it's still being fought in vain today. It's called the war on drugs and addictions. Today, there are millions of people at war with satan over addictions to alcohol and drugs and other sinful behavior around the World! It is a Spiritual War, where our enemy is invisible, "For we wrestle not against flesh and blood, but against principalities, against powers, against the rulers of the darkness of this world, against spiritual wickedness in high places." (Ephesians 6:12) A war without ground troops, tanks, fighter jets, and bombs. The death toll and destruction of this war however, has probably surpassed all the wars of the World between men, since the beginning of time. Yet very little effort is put into conquering it. It lingers on and on and on, year after year after year, with the victims and death tolls rising exponentially, with no end in sight. My prayer is that those who read this book will come away with a better understanding of how Gods Truth applies to their battle with an addiction, and that they will be set free from it! (John 8:31-36) That they will find Victory! (1 Cor. 15:57) Psalm 18:39 says, "You armed me with strength for **battle;** you made my adversaries bow at my feet." Also, in

2 Corinthians 10:4, Paul says, "We use God's mighty weapons, not worldly weapons, to knock down the strongholds of human reasoning and to destroy false arguments." This book shows how "soldiers" for Christ, armed with His Word, The Truth, can win this war with the "Faith of a mustard seed"!

This book is about the dilemma of a silent, deadly, and invisible killer, that's not only out of control, but it has turned into an epidemic around the world today. It's about a plague of drug, alcohol, and other life destroying addictions that's been growing unchecked for so long, it's now eroding the moral fibers of our society! It's an epidemic that no longer has any cultural boundaries! It's as common today in a 30 story office building on Wall Street, as it is in the gutters and alleys of a slum just a few blocks away. It's in every neighborhood, our schools, our factories, our governments, *and* our churches! Rarely does a day go by when there's not a news story about some famous celebrity, politician, sports star, business tycoon, socialite, or popular Church leader, in some type of trouble that can be attributed to drug or alcohol addictions. In spite of addiction recovery programs, treatment facilities, and group homes on every street corner, each of which claim to have the answer to the problem, it just keeps growing out of control. One reason why it's so difficult to control, is because while it kills and maims millions of innocent victims, and ruins the lives of millions of innocent family members, and others in the path of its destruction, at the same time, it's created a billion dollar a year industry that thrives and grows with every new victim.

Just as greed has driven mankind and governments to many wars over the centuries of history, this war is no different. Although It's Spiritual warfare, (Ephesians 6:12), there's still an enemy that's intent on winning at any cost and without any guilt or shame. It's a war man began fighting in the beginning of time, and with the same enemy that originally deceived him in the Garden of Eden. That enemy, or adversary, is satan, the master of deception and lies from that day in the garden, until right this minute! If he could deceive the first two perfectly innocent people God created, imagine what he can do, and *is* doing to us today with all the time he's had to perfect his skills!

Deceiving the average alcoholic or drug addict, once they've become addicted, is a pretty simple task for the master of lies and deceit. The big problem here is the large number of care-givers and "experts" in the secular addiction recovery industry who are being so easily deceived. During the past 50 or more years, thousands of people have decided that they all have *the* answer to the problem. Many *professing* professionals, doctors, and mental health **"experts,"** counselors with office walls plastered with degrees and certificates, claiming to be qualified to "heal", or otherwise restore or cure their $$$$$ "clients"!

All of this delusional "treatment" we're faced with today is pretty much the direct result of one program started about 50 years ago by 2 alcoholic friends who were told by, (I'm assuming a snake oil doctor), that they had an allergy! Yes, that their drunkenness was an allergy! Convinced, (deceived), this to be true, they decided to start a program to share this news with others. Perhaps with good intentions, but nonetheless deceptive results, and for the purpose of recruiting larger numbers, and a broader audience, they proclaimed to be Christians. They obviously had some knowledge of scripture and even some attendance at Christian groups and organizations, and used a few verses here and there to build a following of Christians as well as unbelievers. However, they refused to allow any discussion of Jesus Christ and the Gospel, or any reference to the Cross or Salvation, and they promoted the idea that one could worship **any** God of personal understanding, (or a "higher power as one might understand him"). They also wrote and published their own bible, "The Big Book", and refused to let Gods Word into the meetings. No where did they acknowledge the fundamental doctrine of "The Great Commission," (Matthew 28:16-20). Not only did they build their program on these policies, and refer to them as a 12-step recovery system, but they are still being practiced at meetings around the world today. Today, this practice would immediately be red-flagged as a cult! However, you'll find this group and other 12-step offshoots, widespread in Christian churches everywhere.

    The Truth is, I'm not at all opposed to AA or any of its many offshoots operating in the secular world. I believe they've helped millions of people find sobriety over the years. There is a place and a big need for their service in the secular world. Where I do have a big problem, and am very much opposed to and affronted, is when they are allowed to infiltrate into our Christian churches. When their secular teachings are taught as Christian Truth without question, and in place of Gods Holy Word and Gospel, I have a problem with that! I have a problem with all heresy and blasphemy! This practice should be considered unacceptable in any Christian Church.

    The problem, I believe is that the church, under so much pressure to do *"something"* to address this crisis of addictions, turned to what they thought was the only tool available to them at the time, which may very well have been the case, and without adequate research, allowed secular 12-step addiction recovery programs into their churches. This practice has been going on now in thousands of churches worldwide, for far too long, and is escalating into a debacle that can no longer be accepted or tolerated. Given the fact that the information taught in a secular 12-step addiction recovery program is pure Heresy, It never should have crept into the church to begin with, but the world's deception is our enemies #1 strategy! I'll be discussing the lies and deception used by satan in addiction recovery in our churches in much detail throughout this book.

Later, in another chapter, I will address the 4 fundamental lies of secular 12-step programs and the opposing Truths of God's Word as they apply to addiction recovery. "THE 4 PILLARS OF TRUTH FOR CHRISTIANS IN ADDICTION RECOVERY" was created to be used as a Bible Study based on volumes of scripture. I will also reveal a Christian 12-Truth Bible Study program that also uses volumes of scripture to address issues in more comprehensive detail, the recovery of all forms and types of addictions. It's called the 12 CHRISTIAN TRUTHS AND BIBLE STUDIES FOR ADDICTION RECOVERY, and created to oppose and dispel the lies that so many Christians are used to in their years of studying the secular 12-steps. These programs and much more valuable information relating to Gods Truth in addiction recovery are currently available on my website: www.addictioncrucifixionfellowship.com

In the Christian Church, and according to God's Word, "drunkenness" is Sin. Period. Sin is Sin, and Gods Word and the Holy Spirit is the gift God has blessed us with to overcome it. Scripture is our armor against sin, and the lies and deception of the Devil! (Ephesians 6:10-17) For a Christian to try to beat or conquer the sin of addictions with secular programs, based on mans philosophy, or satan's lies and deception, is like trying to put out a fire with gasoline! It can't be done! For a Christian church to try to mix the teaching of God's Word with secular teaching, is like trying to mix oil and water, it can't be done! And all it will accomplish is to do more damage to those who are the most vulnerable, and who need to hear the Truth the most, and turn them away from the church and God! And, or, keep them in the bondage of the addictions they so desperately need to be set free from.

The Church today is heavily burdened with troubled sheep, and is rampant with false teaching. It's becoming more and more difficult every day to find a Gospel teaching church **centered** on the Cross and Christ's shed blood, and the "washing of feet", rather than washing cars in the parking lot to put new carpet in the chapel. Far too many Christians are growing to believe they can be saved without repenting or forsaking the World. In addiction recovery, there are many, perhaps millions worldwide, who believe they're saved, and can continue to live the same worldly lifestyle of partying, and drinking and doing drugs, and partaking in other Sin, until it grows into an addiction. Then, unfortunately, after they've gotten past the denial stage, and begin looking for help, all they may be able to find is a church with a secular recovery program. A secular 12-step program that's going to tell them that they have an incurable disease instead of Sin, that they're powerless, hopeless, and helpless! And if it's an AA program, they'll be encouraged to worship any god of their choice, "a higher power of their understanding"! Yes, pure Heresy, if those messages are being taught in your Christian Church! A deadly concoction, perhaps more deadly than the addiction they might have!

What's one to do, you might ask, if there are no other programs available at your church? One thing might be to look for another church with a Christ centered, Bible based recovery program, just for the program. I'm not advocating changing churches, just addiction recovery programs where you'll be taught the Truth. Or, if this idea wasn't your first choice, pick up your Bible, get on your knees, and ask God to show you His way to living a changed life. Pastors, counselors, programs, and mentors are all options that may not be available to everyone. God, and His Holy Word are always available, any time, any place, under any circumstance. His promise is written in the Blood of His Lamb, Jesus Christ! And His Promise is that if you have the Faith of a mustard seed, He will move you to the top of this mountain of addiction you've been struggling to climb out from under! Yes, it's more comfortable and convenient to do it in fellowship with others, who can pick us up when we're down, and encourage us to keep going when we don't want to, someone we can call in the middle of a crisis. But we must learn to be cautious in who we fellowship with. We can't let anyone, or any program become a false idol, and lead us away from God. The time we spend doing it alone with God at our side, can have many benefits we can't get in programs. Learning to become completely reliant on Him is exactly what He wants from us in the first place, so the sooner we learn to do so, the sooner we'll start reaping His rewards, and the closer we draw to Him, (James 4:8), the easier it is to hear and understand His voice and instructions. That will help expedite our journey to a full recovery.

    That Faith of a mustard seed will not only grow to allow you to climb to the top of the mountain, but change you into a brand new person in a brand new world! (2 Corinthians 5:17) If you find the journey slow and challenging, I'll offer two encouragements; one, are your knees bleeding? If not, you're not giving your "Utmost for His Highest", remember most of Gods promises are conditional, you have to do your share to receive

His Blessings. And second and finally, if you're still being tested, remember the refiner's fire. (Malachi 3:2) He's perfecting you for a very special purpose. Once you discover that purpose, and begin to live your life in its direction, and in obedience according to His will, you'll be **SAVED** and **SOBER!**

CHAPTER 2

The Many Battlegrounds of Addictions

Psalm 55:18
*"He rescues me unharmed from the **battle** waged against me, even though many oppose me."*

No matter where you are, who you are, what time of day or night it is, or whatever circumstance you're involved in, whether you're at work, at school, at home, on the road, in the grocery store, or at church, on a train, or in an airplane, no matter who, what, where, or when, you're in either the direct, or indirect line of fire of the destruction of someone's battle with addiction. In this, the real world, if your heads not buried in the sand, you're not much more than a stone's throw away from some affect of the War of addiction! You don't even need to step outside your front door to be a victim, someone high on any one of the many poisonous drugs available today, might kick in your front door to rob you, and if your home, they may even hurt you! It's very sad, but very true! The burdens addiction places on our society is staggering. The costs are staggering! Not just the financial costs, which are probably impossible to calculate, and rise uncontrollably every day, but the more important cost is the tax on mankind's emotional and moral values. There is no value we can place on these values. Unless we're Christians, then the value becomes our Salvation. Our moral values are a direct reflection on our sinful nature.

And it's how we deal with our sin that determines our Salvation. We only have 2 choices, Repent, and turn from our sin, or not. We're either obedient to God, or not. Those are very simple and clear choices, yet many choose to ignore them. That's another topic for another chapter, or another book. To be continued….

Back to the battlegrounds,….are you on your way home from work on the freeway? If so, the chances are very good that just ahead of you, or behind you, or beside you is an addict or an alcoholic! Maybe high, and or drunk! Are you in the check-out lane at your local supermarket? Are you on the local bus? Cashing a check at your bank? Having lunch at your favorite diner? Getting gas at the gas station? Are you at work, at school, at the movies, at church, or at home, the chances are that someone within shouting distance is an addict or very close to someone who is. Look around you, do you see them? Chances are you can't. Addiction is usually silent and invisible. Sometimes if you're downtown in the ghetto, driving by an alley, if you're looking, you might spot an alcoholic or an addict. You may, at any time, in any public place, see, smell, or hear an alcoholic or addict. Sometimes their appearance, smell, or slurred talk will give them away. But 90% of the time you won't have a clue when one is sitting or standing next to you.

They all live in the closet of denial, by seclusion and delusion. Millions of alcoholics are able, in the early stages anyways, to get up and go to work in the morning. One may be working right next to you right this minute. Serving you your coffee or breakfast, driving you to work in his cab, cashing your check at the bank, checking out your groceries, taking your order on the phone, selling you or fixing your car at the auto dealership, flying the airplane you're on, at your driver's window handing you a speeding ticket, teaching your child at school, standing in front of you Sunday morning preaching! Maybe even the person behind the bench giving you a 5-year jail sentence for your 10th DUI conviction, or even worse, performing a quadruple bypass heart surgery on you or a loved one! It sounds like a wild stretch of imagination or exaggeration, but you can hear about these stories in the news every day. Any person you come in contact with today, anyplace, at any time, may have just come from the restroom after having a drink of booze or popping a pill or shooting up heroin! You don't know, you won't know, and you can't know, who it might be. It's like Halloween every day, their always wearing a mask or a costume. At best, you might suspect a problem, because of an outward slip on their part, but 99% of the time the Devil is in the details of a well executed cover-up.

The many masks and disguises of denial, delusion, and deception are the addict's next best friend. One minute you might be dealing with a well mannered, articulate, gentleman or lady, who an hour later, turns into a "Jack-the-ripper", or devil in disguise! Their best friend is their drug of choice. At some point nothing else matters. Not family, work, health, and certainly not life, nor God. Only our drug of choice and easy access to it is all that matters. No one should attempt to get between the addict and their drug of choice without confrontation.

This is when we get dragged onto the battleground with them, wherever and whenever the battle rages out of control with an addict, and for whatever reason, we might find Ourselves involuntarily on someone else's battleground. We may become a helpless innocent victim, taken hostage by circumstances beyond our control. In the many halls of Addiction Recovery meetings, there's a saying, "addicts don't make relationships, they take hostages"! Unfortunately, there's a great deal of truth to that cliché.

As you can see the battlegrounds can be anyplace, at any time. Your wildest imagination can't begin to prepare you for the endless circumstances that may entangle you or a loved one or a neighbor into an addict's battle. All of the forests in the world do not have enough trees to produce enough paper to print all the possibilities that exist, but here I'll try to share a few examples that may be more common.

One of the more current and most tragic events our society seems to be facing today, and at an alarming rate of increase, is the number of serious and fatal DUI traffic accidents, by drivers without driver's licenses, and multiple convictions for DUI's. Many of these tragic accidents have been hit and runs. In some cases there have been witnesses who provide authorities with evidence leading to arrests. In many other cases, the killers are still at large, quite possibly still drinking and driving! This epidemic has been growing and growing out of control in this state during the past decade, and this past year it seems there's been a new case reported in the news almost every day. These tragedies affect and create thousands of innocent victims, sometimes hundreds per incident, when you consider the families and friends of all those directly impacted. The bigger tragedy is that our governments, at all levels, seems to have their heads in the sand, and are seemingly doing nothing about this crisis! And then an even greater tragedy, (the crescendo just keeps building), is the fact that the general public seems to have *their* heads buried in the sand also, and refuses to speak out and hold those in power accountable.

Another significant and common battleground, that directly and indirectly affects millions of people in this country alone, is the spiraling crime rate and its many trickle-down consequences due to this out of control epidemic of drug and alcohol abuse. If you're not already somehow affected by crime, you very well might be before the day ends. In reality everyone *is* affected somehow at least indirectly. For example, no one has any privacy anymore, once they step outside their home. Wherever we go, we're on a security camera somewhere. It all started long before terrorism to curb crime. In spite of all these cameras being installed everywhere, the crime rates just keep rising. The prison populations have at least doubled in the past two decades in most states, at a staggering cost to the taxpayers. Most of the increase in prison populations are the addicts and the alcoholics themselves for various related offences. As fast as dealers can come up with new drugs, and ways and means to distribute them, the addicts come up with new crimes or ways to commit old crimes. Modern technology designed to curb crime, only works for a short time until a criminal figures out a way to defeat it. I.D. theft has become a huge problem that's claimed millions of victims recently. So it's easy to see the many millions of victims and hostages claimed on the battleground of the crimes related to addiction and drugs in our country alone, and this is a worldwide event.

    During the past several decades our governments couldn't keep up with the demand to build new prisons and jails to house the increase in population of drug related criminals. Rather than focusing on the problem of rehabilitating repeat offenders, the policies and laws were changed to simply "lock them up, and throw away the keys." Longer and stiffer sentencing guidelines, "we'll just build a new prison or jail and pass the burden on to the taxpayer." In reality, while the prison and jail populations for drug and alcohol related crimes grew exponentially, it's had zero impact on drug and alcohol abuse in this country! In fact drug and alcohol abuse has been, and is still rising exponentially! In the past 2-3 years due to our recent recession, many governments have been forced to close many prisons or jails, or significantly reduce staffing because of budget restraints. Thus, having to release many un-rehabilitated addicts and alcoholics, not to mention child molesters and bank robbers, back into society early, into parole programs that are "under staffed" and over-burdened.

"The writing on the wall" tells us that we have a huge, out of control problem here that has no where's to go! In spite of the recent growth in traditional secular drug and alcohol recovery programs and treatment facilities there's been no impact on reducing the spiraling out of control growth. So if the Government can't control or "fix" the problem, and the secular recovery industry, with its philosophical 12-step programs, has had little if any impact on reducing the problem, what other choice do we have?

What choice do we have to end this insanity? We have the same choice today that we've had since the beginning of time. Turn to, and surrender our lives and wills over to The Almighty God, and His Son Jesus Christ, be "set free", and be **"SAVED and SOBER"**!

CHAPTER 3

The Many Weapons of the Enemy

John 18:3 NIV,
So Judas came to the grove, guiding a detachment of soldiers and some officials from the chief priests and Pharisees. They were carrying torches, lanterns and weapons.

In Spiritual warfare, satan, our adversary, has an arsenal full of many weapons. As Christians, our Salvation is satan's number one target. He does not want us to succeed and will stop at nothing to keep us from Eternal Life with God. Satan has a couple of weapons of ***mass destruction***, literally! Addiction and deception! First, ***addiction*** to drugs, alcohol, and other destructive behavior, (sin), is in itself, one of satan's many weapons to keep man from Salvation. Not only is drug and alcohol addiction a spiritual war raging within many of us, but at the same time it's a weapon of war he uses to keep us from God, and Salvation. I believe addiction is his number one first choice of weapons. Since it affects millions of people every day around the world, it is clearly without a doubt, "a weapon of mass destruction"! If you add all the lives it's claimed or destroyed since the Garden, it far surpasses the death tolls and destruction of all the wars, atom bombs, plagues, and holocausts during the same period of time. Millions of people right this very minute around the world are suffering in many different ways, from many different types of addictions! Millions of other innocent victims, codependents, friends and loved ones, directly and indirectly are suffering right this very minute as a result of the actions of an addict or an alcoholic.

How indirectly can it be? As infinite as your imagination will allow you to wander! Let my imagination take you on an imaginable sample journey of potential possibilities. Then use your own imagination, if you care to, to think of a few other examples you might already know about, or have heard about. The chances are you can think of many scenarios you might even be personally familiar with. Again, we're looking for an example of someone's pain and suffering as the indirect result of an addicts dysfunctional behavior. Perhaps the owner of a business where you've worked for the past 20 years, was sentenced to 10 years in prison for a drunk driving accident resulting in a fatal traffic accident, and you didn't even know your boss had a drinking problem, he hid it well. Now the business will have to close and the other 10 employees will also be out of work. Some may lose their homes, others may have to move to find work, and others may lose their health insurance, and on and on goes the possibilities of trickle-down effects to millions of innocent victims affected by one person's undetected drunkenness. One person's total enslavement to the bondage of sin. One attack by satan affecting hundreds of people. So one incident of alcohol abuse gone unchecked, can affect potentially hundreds of innocent bystanders! I could go on and on and on with an infinite list of similar stories and tragedies, but this one, and other similar stories are repeated almost every minute somewhere in this country.

Before I leave this topic, another important

element of this problem, is the fact that in many of the above scenarios, such as fatal DUI's, the "killers," and that's exactly what they are, often have multiple DUI convictions, yet are still driving for whatever reason. In this state, there's been a huge increase recently in the number of hit-and-runs,(often resulting in fatalities), yet the news media seems to be oblivious to questioning the "why" for this senseless uptick in manslaughter? I'm sure if they researched the facts, they would discover that in most cases these drivers were drunk! If they don't get caught for a day or two, the authorities can't prosecute for DUI, because the blood levels return to normal, and tests are inconclusive. Without tougher DUI laws, and enforcement of the current laws, this problem will only continue to escalate as it's been doing for years.

Why? There are a number of reasons, but the primary one is that the lawmakers in this country have become "soft" on alcoholics, and DUI's. They're soft on drugs and drug trafficking, and to save money on enforcement, they've legalized drugs in many states because the "users" have convinced them "that it's good for their health"! And we just keep electing these fools to protect us! They're soft on drug and alcohol recovery programs, convinced that addicts and alcoholics have a disease, so the insurance industry should be responsible for their "healthcare." Just try convincing the government these people have a sin problem, not an allergy!

In spite of the billions of dollars spent over the past few decades, on "the war on drugs," and on recovery programs, the only results seem to be a 10-fold *increase* in the spread of this plague! No one in the government will take any responsibility, and the silence in the government speaks volumes to their obvious total disconnect to the problem. I believe they've just given up. Historically, they know there's been little if any progress made in spite of their futile efforts at curbing drug and alcohol abuse in the past few decades, so they've thrown in the towel and silently proclaimed defeat!

Most of the blame for the above problems with addictions in this country and around the world, can be attributed to satans second weapon of mass destruction which is deception! Jeremiah 9:6 says, "You live in the midst of deception; in their deceit they refuse to acknowledge me," declares the Lord. Deception is a silent and invisible killer! It is our adversary's, (satans), number two weapon of mass destruction! Right behind addiction. It has lead millions over the cliff straight into hell! The enemy uses it to hide and veil addiction and all other sin. The wiles, (cunningness), of our enemy are many, and if we don't seek Gods Truth with great vigor, the devil will succeed at leading us astray! In this day and age we must remain vigilant at all times, becoming like the Bereans, (Acts 17:11), and closely examining the scripture daily, and comparing it to what we're hearing and reading. Knowing that much of the deception coming from the enemy today, is coming directly from many pulpits!

Satan used deception to trick Adam and Eve in the Garden, in, Genesis 3:4-5, "You will not surely die," the serpent said to the woman, "For God knows that when you eat of it your eyes will be opened, and you will be like God, knowing good and evil." The only thing that's changed since then, is satin's been busy honing his skills in deceiving us, while we, (mankind), have been asleep at the wheel, (trying to reinvent it I guess)! More than likely he's used it today, on you and I in some way or another, in our sinful nature. While addiction is one weapon he'll use to keep us from Salvation, deception, is a weapon he can use in all the other battles with other sin we find ourselves fighting with throughout the day. When we fall short and give in to the temptation of greed, pride, lust, or lying, he'll be right there to deceive us with similar words of deception as those he used in the garden, in Genesis 3:1, "Did God **really** say you must not eat the fruit from any of the trees in the garden?" Did he *really* say that a *little* lie here and there will hurt, or a *little* pride, or lust or greed is sin, and will keep you from Heaven? *Surely* God wouldn't be that mean and unloving.

    This type of deception is rotting the core of Christianity. Christians have become so deceived and confused during the past few decades, because of false teaching, and lack of teaching the Truth, many have no idea what Salvation is, or means to them, or what they need to do to acquire it. Many, perhaps millions, are under the understanding that all they need to do to be saved, is "be a good person." One very important Truth rarely shared from the pulpit today, is that most of Gods promises are "conditional". One popular context of verses heard frequently to describe our "freedom" in Christ, is John 8:31-32, when Jesus says, "To the Jews who had believed him, Jesus said, "If you hold to my teaching, you are really my disciples. 32 Then you will know the truth, and the truth will set you free." The *condition* here being, "***If,***" you hold to my teaching," but many miss that *condition*, and expect to be "set free" without "*holding to His teachings*".

    This is only one of many promises throughout His Word that come with certain conditions or expectations from God. Many professing Christians today see God as some kind of Santa Claus. Out of sheer ignorance, greed, and selfishness, they expect God to deliver on all his promises, in *their* time frame, without any conditions. Why should they have to repent to be Saved? They've become so deceived, the enemy's turned them into "cultural Christians", believing they can pray a simple prayer, and be saved, without forsaking the world.

It's all of this *deception* that satans been using forever, that keeps us in our *addictions,* if we let him, by not paying close attention to God's Word. By not reading the Bible ourselves, for guidance and direction, instead, we tend to listen to another man's reading and interpretation of it, as the Truth, as it applies to us. This book was written for the express purpose of trying to reveal the many lies and deceptions satan's been quite successfully using, specifically during the past few decades, to keep Christians in the dark when it comes to the Truth about addiction recovery.

Secular addiction recovery programs don't apply to Christians, and don't belong in Christian churches, PERIOD!!!!! And yet thousands of churches around the world today use secular addiction recovery programs to minister to and counsel Christians who are fighting this Spiritual warfare with satan over addictions. Secular recovery programs don't consider drunkenness as Sin, but refer to it as a disease. I'll explain this lie, and many more lies that satan is using to deceive the Christian and His church, in much detail throughout this book. Life, without God in it, is a very dark and painful place. This emptiness can quickly overcome us with depression, anger, fear, loneliness, and sadness. Since alcohol and drugs are first and foremost a pain-killer, alcoholics and drug addicts find great relief and escape from the reality of that pain and loneliness, by consuming as much alcohol or drugs as they need to cover it up and escape from it. Instead of turning to God to fill that void in their Heart, and turn the pain into joy, peace, and Love, satan convinces them that, "***surely*** a little alcohol or narcotic or other sin, won't hurt, in fact it will make you feel good!" Since the alcohol or drugs, or the pleasure from other sin wears off in a short while, the pain and depression quickly returns, and the cycle begins all over again.

Deception, deception, deception, it's everywhere, and without God in our lives to guide us, we wouldn't be able to see it, or recognize it, if it bit us. Psalm 25:5, "guide me in your **Truth** and teach me, for you are God my Savior, and my hope is in you all day long". A big problem today, is that the devils deception isn't just on the street corner, or in the world and worldly places and events. It's not just keeping *unbelievers* lost and facing Eternal damnation, but it's everywhere we go, including many of our churches! Many of our churches are filled with "church-goers", who do not have God in their Hearts guiding them towards the Truth! Nor will they find it in a church that's not teaching it. We are all vulnerable no matter who we are, or where we go to church! Yes, a very bold accusation, however, a very sad Truth, and one that everyone needs to hear! Not just hear, but think about, pray about, and take action over. "The Truth will set you free!" Lies will not.

Again, we all need to become like the Bereans, (Acts 17:11), and read the scripture daily, to check and verify that everything which we've seen, read or heard in church, or on TV, or in a book like this, is exactly what God said in His Holy Word! Yes, I would encourage every reader of *this* book to take the time to verify its contents with God's Word. On my website, www.addictioncrucifixionfellowship.com, I use volumes of scripture to back my writings and they're all linked directly to another website with the Bible scripture just a click away, in many different translations and languages for verification and comparison. We must take the time to examine all this scripture *in context,* not just one verse from here and there by itself. This is the only way we can be assured that we're being taught Gods Truth and living righteously, instead of being deceived. And to be assured that satan's behind us, and not in front of us, leading us straight to Hell!

Almost every one of the original writers of the Bible speaks of the importance of being aware of false teachers and prophets and their lies and deception. One of my favorite places in scripture on the topic of false teachers is in Galatians 1:8-9, where the Apostle Paul, clearly very frustrated with the church in Galatia says, "But even if we or an angel from heaven should preach a gospel other than the one we preached to you, let him be eternally condemned! As we have already said, so now I say again: If anybody is preaching to you a gospel other than what you accepted, let him be eternally condemned!" (NIV) Clearly Paul was very upset with not only the false teachers, but with the church as well. We, (the church) today, need to take a stand against the many false teachers, teachings, and cults that are corrupting, not only the Christian Church today, but the Christians in them!

One of the biggest problems in the church today, throughout the world, is the idea that scripture like this doesn't apply to Christians today! That somehow Gods Word is no longer valid, or no longer the Truth! No longer relevant! That, "Oh, I believe in God, but I don't believe that this verse applies to me, or this situation!" Or, "But because I believe in God and I'm a good person, I must be a Christian and be saved!" Or, "pray this simple prayer and be saved." "Prayer" does not save, "Faith" saves, "through Grace." I've heard these statements a million times in the past few years, much to my frustration. Not towards the lost souls making them, but a growing frustration towards the false teachers who, over the years have been deceiving the multitudes into believing such nonsense! "We should be telling it like it is, in the vernacular, so people can understand it, or don't tell it at all!" And, as you'll discover throughout this book, my frustration with false teachers and teachings as they apply to Christians in addiction recovery, is the inspiration God's blessed me with to write this book. To share with the readers His Truths, and expose satan's lies and deception, as they apply to a Christian's recovery.

A third weapon in the enemy's arsenal is denial, the definition being, regarding our state of mind, "a refusal or an inability to recognize and deal with a serious personal problem or refusal to face unpleasant facts." Regarding addictions, denial is rejecting the idea, or refusing to accept the truth that we have a problem with addictions. An inability to recognize that we're in total bondage or enslaved to whatever sin it might be that is controlling or dominating our life. Whether it's drugs or alcohol, sex or pornography, gambling or over-eating, once it reaches the point where we can't control it, it becomes an addiction to this sin. Once we say "we don't have a problem with it," we're in "denial," and that's when the real battle begins!

No matter what the world's definition of denial is, the root cause of it, is "pride." And pride is sin, Psalm 10:4, "In his pride the wicked does not seek him; in all his thoughts there is no room for God." So you end up with sin taking charge over another sin. A "lose - lose" combination. Adam first exposed us to the sin of pride in the garden, when he covered himself with fig leaves because he was embarrassed and ashamed for disobeying God, only to further his predicament, and digging a deeper hole for himself, giving us our first example of denial, by denying his fault, and blaming Eve for the circumstances they found themselves in.

This is so true of addicts and alcoholics today. A big part of denial is to blame someone else. ***Anyone*** else, before taking any of the responsibility themselves. This can almost become an indefinable form of insanity amongst addicts, who seemingly would rather OD, or drink themselves to death, than admit they have a problem that they can't fix! Proverbs 16:18, "Pride goes before destruction, a haughty spirit before a fall." One common factor among everyone who suffers from addictions, is that no-one can start on the road to recovery until they've overcome denial. Until they've taken full responsibility for their actions. Actions that have caused much pain and suffering throughout their families, have destroyed relationships and marriages, actions that have caused many to lose homes, jobs, business', much wealth, and health. Hopefully, you will reach the threshold of exiting denial, and enter into reality and recovery, before you have to lose every-thing dear and precious to you, including your very life. Unfortunately however, many never step out of denial into reality, and end up dying in their sin, only to spend eternity in Hell with the one they've been sleeping with all along!

    To them, may they wake up to the Truth, before it's too late, may they see beyond their pride and see the pain on their loved ones faces, and their broken hearts, may they understand that there's always Hope in Jesus, and that He is the only way out of this living Hell of addictions they've found themselves stuck in! May they turn to God, who they've been running from all their lives, before it's too late.

    To them, may they understand that addictions destroy human life to the core. It starts in the Heart and grows outward, like a cancer destroying all of mans emotions and hope, until there's nothing left but the ashes of hell! It destroys one's ability to Love or Hope, to feel pain or sorrow or joy, to grow and mature, to have relationships with others, or to dream. It eventually destroys the mind and finally the body. If we don't allow God to intervene before the latter stages of this decay, we'll miss the opportunity to live an abundant life with Him here and now, and possibly miss the chance for eternal life with Him. I believe an addict or an alcoholic can reach a point of no return. Yes, the thief on the cross with Jesus was saved at the last minute, but scripture suggests he was coherent. However, should an addict or an alcoholic linger in their sin until it destroys the brain, and renders them permanently **incoherent**, short of a miracle of Jesus raising them from being "brain dead", it would be too late to change the path their on. Once we've crossed the threshold of denial into reality, we can begin to move forward and become **SAVED and SOBER!**

And finally a fourth, and very "cunning" weapon in the devil's arsenal, used to keep one paralyzed in addiction, is "enabling." It's next to impossible to recognize or understand, without thoughtful study and close examination. Anyone reading this out of compassion for a loved one, a friend, or a suffering church member, or the addicts themselves that might be reading this, and searching for "triggers" and causes for their addictions, must learn to recognize the many elements of enabling. We must learn how they work to keep an alcoholic or an addict in their addictions, if they or the enabler want to learn how to **"*disable"*** the enabler! Proverbs 19:18 says, "Discipline your son, for in that there is hope; do not be a willing party to his death."

To enable someone in their addictions, will lead to many ***"disabling"*** consequences. Not all addicts become addicts with someone else's help. Many need no help whatsoever. But many more get lots of help without even asking for it. Enabling is almost always provided with good intentions, and while most often supplied by family members, they get lots of help from friends, family, classmates, co-workers, and even employers! And on almost every occasion, the enabler doesn't have a clue what they're doing. That they're helping their loved one stay enslaved to their addiction. At least in the beginning, they don't know their friend or loved one or colleague has a problem, and is digging themselves, (and often others), a very deep hole. And then when they do begin to smell a fish, it's often too late, or they're afraid to say no for a variety of wrong reasons. This scenario plays out a million times a day as far as the East is from the West! One phone call at a time, "Hi Mom, can you help me with $20 bucks"? "Hi Sis, can you loan me a few bucks till next week"? "Hey Billy, can you help me with my rent money for a week"? Or, "honey, can you call my boss and tell him I'm sick"? It goes on and on, over and over again, one phone call at a time, for what begins to seem like eternity, until one day you get that dreaded phone call that your loved one is in jail or detox, or worse, maybe MUCH worse! And then the first question you ask is, "If I only knew"! A feasible comment for many, but a poor excuse for many others, with their heads in the sand, who may have been ignoring a problem of a loved one or friend for years. I believe its human nature for most of us to, "mind my own business", turn the other way and ignore the problem! Then, when the problem escalates into a tragedy, we blame ourselves.

    Another common "breeding ground" if you will, for enabling, outside of the home, and yet close to everyone concerned, might be in the church, when a hard-working, devoted husband, and loving father, and church member, stumbles into the pastors office one day admitting an addiction! It doesn't matter if it's a tiny little country church in a town of 500, or a giant, big city mega-church with thousands of members and a huge staff, *few* are equipped to handle this kind of tragedy adequately! Not only is addiction a tragedy, but it's also become in recent years an epidemic! Why are most churches ill-equipped to handle such vital, potentially deadly circumstances? For one thing, the church itself, in many cases has been in denial of the problem, or certainly the magnitude of the problem, until recently when it grew into such an epidemic, they could no longer ignore it. Then, 90% of the folks in your church who might have a problem with an addiction are in denial themselves, so you have a much bigger problem than you can begin to imagine. If denial is a form of blindness, which it is, you have the blind leading the blind.

Enabling in the church or the Christian home is extremely difficult to recognize and address. Since the very foundation of Christianity is based on Love, and enabling is often done "out of Love." How does one convince a Christian mom or dad, brother or sister, child or friend that he or she needs to stop showing so much love to their loved one? How do you tell a loving Christian Mom that they shouldn't bail their son or daughter out of jail again, or pay for another treatment facility or program, or give them more money for the rent, when in reality, it will just go to buy more drugs? That instead, they need to show a form of "hard Love." That they need to stop "giving in," which is a form of "feeding the fire," and will only lead their loved one deeper into the swamp of "quicksand" that they're already stuck in. Or how do you tell them that they need to let their son or daughter, or other loved one, hit rock bottom before they can begin to see the light, and start the long slow process of crawling out of this deep, dark abyss they've been stuck in. This scenario is played out thousands of times every day around the country. And it develops a huge problem that only God, through much prayer and Faith, can resolve. Man alone in this situation is helpless without God!

When addictions leach their way into a Christian family, it can be 10 times more devastating and deadly than when present in the home of unbelievers. Not only will the addicted party be affected, but everyone involved may start asking the age old question when trials show up, "Why God"? And then start to blame God. For many Christians, who fail to rely completely on God for His Divine intervention, this can quickly begin to erode their Faith. As in any and all trials, we need to learn to turn them over to God, and completely trust in Him, and understand that He will turn them into something good! Trials build our faith. (James 1:2-12, 1 Peter 4:12-13) While the pain, suffering and devastation experienced among everyone involved, the addicted, as well as everyone in their path, is equal, the unbeliever has no God to blame. Many have their false gods to blame, and that within itself will keep them entrapped in their addictions. And the Christian who blames and questions his God for his trials, will also remain entrapped in his trials until he learns to trust his God in all things.

Recognizing enabling is difficult because addictions can often be a silent and invisible problem, sometimes well masked and disguised by the addict until it's so far out of control, that when it is finally discovered or revealed, it's a shock to everyone involved. Many times hidden and unknown addictions are revealed through an unexpected tragedy, such as someone ending up in jail or a serious accident, or the loss of a job. The spouse, or co-worker, or friend claims to have had no idea that so-and-so had a problem with an addiction. These are just a few of the many examples of sudden discovery of problems that might have been hidden and undetected for years. These are just some of the many obstacles facing a Pastor or church counselor today. While there can be many obvious warning signs, more often than not, God, a pastor or a counselor, are usually the last ones the addict or alcoholic will reach out to. It's often understood within the family circle, that this is to be a "family secret." As long as it remains to be a secret, it will never be resolved, and will just continue to grow. As long as the addict or alcoholic remains in denial, he'll keep everyone around him hostage to the idea that he doesn't have a problem, that they need to cooperate with him to keep him out of trouble, and keep the situation under control. As long as the enablers agree to this insanity, the addict will continue on this merry-go-round and around until it goes over a cliff.

    What choice do we have to end this insanity? We have the same choice today that we've had since the beginning of time. Turn to, and surrender our lives and wills over to The Almighty God, and His Son Jesus Christ, be "set free", and be **"SAVED and SOBER"!**

CHAPTER 4

Be born Again

(John 3:3)
"I tell you the truth; no one can see the kingdom of
God unless he is born again".

**RISE OUT OF THE DEEP, DARK ABYSS
OF ADDICTIONS, INTO THE LIGHT!**

Psalm 89:15
Blessed are those who have learned to acclaim you,
who walk in the light of your presence, Lord.

The beginning of the rest of our lives starts when we step over the threshold of denial, into reality as exposed by the Truth. Admitting that our sinful nature, led by satan, has been dominating, ruling, and ruining our life, and every aspect and element of it, since the day we were born and began walking, talking, and thinking. We've decided, perhaps through Gods conviction that we need to turn that control over to God. We're no longer holding onto the worldly pleasures of the sins we were addicted to. Whatever they might have been, we're done with them. We've left them in the toy box, (2 Tim. 2:22), and turned from them, and towards God, repenting and nailing our sin to the cross (Colossians 2:13-14), with His Son, Jesus!

Surrendering completely to His Love and will for us. For the Christian, this total surrender is known as "being born again." (John 3:3)

For the Christian struggling with addictions, who's just crossed the threshold of denial, John 3:3, "being born again", is the one step to Eternal Life and everlasting addiction recovery. The born again Christian needs no further steps, as they become brand new creatures in Christ, (2 Cor. 5:17), and God immediately begins the process of sanctification, which includes the various actions performed in 12-step recovery programs. We don't sanctify ourselves, God does it for us. (1 Thessalonians 5:23, 1 Cor. 1:30, 1 Peter 1:2) Sanctification is His way of perfecting and molding us into His righteousness. By definition, according to Easton's Bible Dictionary; "Sanctification involves more than a mere moral reformation of character, brought about by the power of the truth: it is the work of the Holy Spirit bringing the whole nature more and more under the influences of the new gracious principles implanted in the soul in regeneration. In other words, sanctification is the carrying on to perfection the work begun in regeneration, and it extends to the whole man (Rom. 6:13; 2 Cor. 4:6; Col. 3:10; 1 John 4:7; 1 Cor. 6:19). It is the special office of the Holy Spirit in the plan of redemption to carry on this work (1 Cor. 6:11; 2 Thess. 2:13). Faith is instrumental in securing sanctification, inasmuch as it secures union to Christ (Gal. 2:20), and brings the believer into living contact with the truth, whereby he is led to yield obedience "to the commands, trembling at the threatenings, and embracing the promises of God for this life and that which is to come."

"Perfect sanctification is not attainable in this life (1 Kings 8:46; Prov. 20:9; Eccl. 7:20; James 3:2; 1 John 1:8). See Paul's account of himself in Rom. 7:14-25; Phil. 3:12-14; and 1 Tim. 1:15; also the confessions of David (Ps. 19:12, 13; 51), of Moses (90:8), of Job (42:5, 6), and of Daniel (9:3-20). "The more holy a man is, the more humble, self-renouncing, self-abhorring, and the more sensitive to every sin he becomes, and the more closely he clings to Christ. The moral imperfections which cling to him he feels to be sins, which he laments and strives to overcome. Believers find that their life is a constant warfare, and they need to take the kingdom of heaven by storm, and watch while they pray. They are always subject to the constant chastisement of their Father's loving hand, which can only be designed to correct their imperfections and to confirm their graces. And it has been notoriously the fact that the best Christians have been those who have been the least prone to claim the attainment of perfection for themselves.", Hodge's Outlines.

Many people believe that they're Christians long before this Spiritual rebirth takes place, having at some previous time, been "led to the Lord" by praying a prayer of Salvation, or perhaps having been baptized by water, possibly as a child. Still many others believe they're saved simply because they grew up "in the church" with their family. These things do not save us, the scripture is clear that Salvation comes by Grace *through* Faith, "For it is by grace you have been saved, through faith—and this not from yourselves, it is the gift of God" (Eph. 2:8), also, "That if you confess with your mouth, "Jesus is Lord," and believe in your heart that God raised him from the dead, you will be saved." (Romans 10:9).

Some people spend many years, while others spend complete lifetimes calling themselves Christians, thinking that they're saved, only because Gods Truth has never been shared with them. It's never been explained to them, that scripture such as John 3:3, (being born again), Eph. 2:8, Romans

10:9, and many more, are essential and vital to their Salvation, and that their relationship with God is in direct proportion to their understanding of His Word. Studying His Word is essential in their ability to grow and mature spiritually allowing them to recognize His will for their lives.

(Hebrews 5:11-13) Those who linger behind in their growth and Spiritual maturity miss out on His full blessings for their life.

To be born again we must develop a close and intimate personal relationship with our Lord and Savior. One in which we not only hear clearly and frequently, His soft and still voice, but actually feel His breath on the back of our neck! We need to be able to know Jesus as our best friend in order to understand what He expects from us. We need to know what He means when He says we must,… "If you refuse to take up your cross and follow me, you are not worthy of being mine." (Matthew 10:38) If we're not giving Him our utmost in return for His Sacrifice for us on the Cross, we're being disrespectful towards Him, and shouldn't be surprised if we're not receiving His utmost for us. If we're burdened and overwhelmed with trials, tribulations, and turbulence in our lives, we should examine and re-evaluate our relationship and commitment to Him.

There are millions in the church today who have been mislead into believing the lie that since Christ set us free from the Law, (Romans 8:2), that obedience to God and His Word is now an option. They somehow believe that sin will be overlooked, since the church itself has begun to tolerate so much of it. Repentance has become a thing of the past, and rarely, if ever mentioned at all in today's modern "new age" church. Yes we are all, each and every one of us are sinners. 1 John 1:10, "If we claim we have not sinned, we make him out to be a liar and his word has no place in our lives.", is a common verse used to prove that we're sinners, and all too often used by many to justify their sin! Rarely do we hear in response to that excuse to justify sin, 1 John 2:4, "The man who says, "I know him," but does not do what he commands is a liar, and the truth is not in him." If we're busy using scripture like 1 john 1:10, and spending our time searching for more scriptural excuses, which there are many, to justify our sin, then we are not Born Again!

Being Born Again is a spiritual, emotional, and conscious change of heart, and recognition of Gods sacrifice for us at Calvary! It's recognizing and appreciating His death on the Cross for us that leads us to complete repentance, a willingness and desire to obediently serve Him, and fulfill His will for us. If we're truly born again, we'll no longer seek excuses to disobey Him, and then make more excuses for doing so by twisting His Word to justify the offence. In other words, "the devil made me do it" is quoted in a thousand different variations. Instead, we'll humbly and willingly seek to show our Savior our Love for Him through our utmost obedience and service to Him. We'll gladly choose to die to self, that we might live for Him. (Gal. 2:20, Phil. 1:21) When we're Born Again, we know it! We know we've changed. The world has become a different place that we don't recognize any more, and we navigate through it differently than we did yesterday. Not only do *we* recognize the change in ourselves, but the world around *you* see's the change. "What happened to you?" Or, "There's something different about you," will be something you should hear repeatedly after you've been Born Again. The change will be undeniable and perfectly clear to you. If you're not sure that you've been Born Again, you're probably not! If we are, we will have full confidence of it, and not question it. (1 John 3:21, 4:17, 5:14)

According to J.C.Ryle; "To be born again is, as it were, to enter upon a new existence, to have a new mind and a new heart, new views, new principles, new tastes, new affections, new likings and new dislikings, new fears, new joys, new sorrows, new love to things once hated, new hatred to things once loved, new thoughts of God and ourselves and the world and the life to come, and the means whereby that life is attained. And it is indeed a true saying that he who has gone through it is a new man, a new creature, for old things are passed away—behold, he can say, all things are become new! It is not so much that our natural powers and faculties are taken away and destroyed; I would rather say that they receive an utterly new bias and direction. It is not that the old metal is cast aside—but it is melted down and refined and remolded, and has a new stamp impressed upon it, and thus, so to speak, becomes a new coin. He goes on to say, "To be born again is to become a member of a new family by adoption, even the family of God; it is to feel that God is indeed our Father, and that we are made the very sons and daughters of the Almighty; it is to become the citizen of a new state, to cast aside the bondage of Satan and live as free men in the glorious liberty of Christ's kingdom, giving our King the tribute of our best affection, and believing that He will keep us from all evil. To be born again is a spiritual resurrection, a faint likeness indeed of the great change at last—but still a likeness; for the new birth of a man is a passage from death to life; it is a passage from ignorance of God to a full knowledge of Him, from slavish fear to childlike love, from sleepy carelessness about Him to fervent desire to please Him, from lazy indifference about salvation to burning, earnest zeal; it is a passage from strangeness towards God to heartfelt confidence, from a state of enmity to a state of peace, from worldliness to holiness, from an earthly, sensual, man-pleasing state of mind to the single-eyed mind that is in Christ Jesus. And this it is to be born of the Spirit." - J.C. Ryle (1816-1900)

Born Again Christians rarely need an introduction! Especially brand new born again believers! Most of those that I've been blessed to meet over the years, have a radiant joyful glow about them that sets them apart from unbelievers. Jesus' presence in their lives is usually obvious simply through their greeting to you. You can see Jesus in their smiles, the sparkle in their eyes, and the joy in their voices! Their obvious Love for their Savior is contagious. Because of their gratitude and newfound freedom from the burden of their sin, and the knowledge of their forgiveness and Salvation, you cannot mistake the indisputable sincerity and genuine Love for Jesus, and His presence in their lives. You can see His reflection in them. Have you ever been there? Does this describe you in the past?

Unfortunately, many of us can relate to "having been there," and wonder what happened? For some of us our relationship with Jesus may have "cooled off" over time. Hopefully not to the point of being "lukewarm," if so, we'll be discussing that condition later in another chapter. The point here is that the "cooling off" of our relationship with Jesus, is not unlike what most of us experience when we're first married, or at the birth of our first child. We're in total ecstasy, and filled emotionally with overwhelming joy and love, and excited just to be alive, at first. Then in time, that initial fire cools off, we begin to get comfortable, and the original excitement begins to wear off, unless we make a conscious effort to keep it alive. To keep the fire alive in our relationship with Jesus, we must constantly feed our Faith with His Word, The Truth. We must continue to grow closer to Him, and never allow ourselves to drift away. Everything else in this world, except Gods Love, will erode eventually! When we've reached this knowledge and stage in our relationship with Him, we know and can be confident that we're "Born Again."

Typically, the most memorable moments in any person's life are those of their weddings, children's births, graduations, then *their* children's weddings, and births of grandchildren. For many of us our "born again experience" is right up there with those exciting memories. Unfortunately, however, for many more of us, if we don't stay intimately close in our relationship with Jesus, it may cool off, and become just a "memory," rather than a continuous ongoing event. Just like our weddings and marriages to our spouses, the excitement can wear off if we don't stay intimately close in our relationship with them. The "on fire for the Lord" flame has flickered from an inferno, to a mere pilot light. Our excitement over our Salvation has dimmed as satan keeps chipping away at our Faith. One trial after another, without an adequate feeding of the Truth, will eventually destroy the Faith of a born again Christian. For some, it may take many years, and the pilot light may never go out, but for others it may not take that long, and for still others, relighting the pilot light may become impossible. That is a topic for another chapter. Be assured however, becoming a "lukewarm" Christian, is not a problem you want to have with God. (Revelation 3:14-22)

There are millions of professing Christians today around the world, who may or may not be born again, but clearly have not been taught Gods Truth. Sadly, most churches today are misleading their members with many different lies, and watered down Truth. You've seen and heard about many of them, the many cults, and many mega-churches with fallen leaders and various scandals over the years. Leaders can only fall when they wander from the Truth! Unfortunately, they take their sheep with them in most cases. The largest church in the world gets more negative media airtime than politics, yet millions flock to it with open wallets because they've been lead to believe they can "buy" their salvation or blessings, or healings! The deception is so thick, yet transparent, if one knows the Truth. It's like bullet proof glass, because satan is a master at hiding the Truth from those who are seeking it. God's Word is more powerful, but one has to know it, and have Faith in it, for them to be able to have victory over satans deception.

One of the biggest lies being taught to, and accepted by millions of believers in my lifetime, is that Christ came to abolish the old-testament law, consequently freeing them from the consequences of sin. (Acts 13:38-40, Romans 8:1-3, 1 Corinthians 9:20-22) Giving the wrong idea that we no longer need to be obedient to God. There is rarely a message today from the pulpit on repentance. That to be "set free" from our sin is a ***conditional*** promise, that "***If you hold to my teaching***, you will be set free." We must repent to be saved, and to repent, we must be ***obedient*** to His will for us. The primary message of the many "name-it-and-claim-it" churches that have become so popular, is "you bless us, and God will bless you back". And if you're not being blessed enough, or you're in a trial, "bless us some more"! The church that teaches the Truth about repentance, and being obedient, picking up our cross and serving others, and other basic Truths, will not be successful, if success is based on attendance numbers and the size of the bank accounts. It will be successful, based on genuine Salvation.

When we become Born Again, out of our Love and respect for Jesus, because of what He's done for us on the cross, we choose to make every effort we can to become obedient to His will for us. Not only do we enter into the process of sanctification, but when we do fall short and sin, we pick ourselves back up, repent, and move forward with more determination and confidence to not let it happen again. Sometimes, some of us have to do it over and over and over again until *He* knows, we know! Until *He* knows we've got it right, and are ready to move on to the next lesson, the next step in the process of sanctification, righting us for our Eternal journey with Him.

Now that we're confident of our Salvation, of who we are in Christ, and know that we're Born Again, we're ready to "be set free" according to John 8:31-36. This is a conditional promise from God, as many are, requiring our obedience, Faith, and service to receive. We'll be discussing this in the next chapter.

What choice do we have to receive God's Blessings? We have the same choice today, that we've had since the beginning of time. Turn to, and surrender our lives and wills over to The Almighty God, and His Son Jesus Christ, be obedient, be "set free", and be **"SAVED and SOBER"**!

CHAPTER 5

Be Set Free

John 8:31-32
"If you hold to my teaching, you are really my disciples. 32 Then you will know the truth, and the truth will set you free."

Once we've been Born Again and become a brand new creation, 2 Corinthians 5:17, "Therefore, if anyone is in Christ, he is a new creation; the old has gone, the new has come", the first and most important thing we need to do is become involved in a good, solid, Christ centered, Bible based Church. This is no easy task, and must be taken very seriously, and done with much prayer, in today's world of false teachings and cults. The biggest obstacle you'll encounter in your new life with Christ, will be Satan, our enemy, he does not want you here! You're probably here, reading this right now, because he's been chasing after your soul with drug and alcohol abuse most of your life, and he certainly doesn't want you turning to Christ for Salvation or recovery from your addictions! You can count on his tricks, lies, deception, and trials in an attempt to discourage you, wear you down, and lead you astray. But more importantly, through the indwelling of the Holy Spirit, you can count on GOD'S Love, Grace and Power, to protect you and carry you through your trials with the Faith of a mustard seed, to Victory over satan in these battles of Spiritual Warfare! In Acts 1:8 Jesus tells us that when we're Born Again, we receive the Holy Spirit and are filled with His Power.

There are many Christians whose souls maybe

saved, but have yet to discover the blessings and free gifts that come with salvation. They've yet to discover scripture that declares their freedom from the bondage of addictions. They're still in denial of their addictions and sinful nature, and of the fact that God's Word is the absolute Truth! John 14:6, Jesus answered, "I am the way and the truth and the life. No one comes to the Father except through me." They're not willing to believe or trust that scripture like John 8:31-36, and Gal. 5:1 applies to them, and that they've been "set free" from the bondage of addiction and sin. If we're born again, we're set free! How do we know? The Bible, God's Word, tells us so! John 8:31-36, 31, Jesus said to the people who believed in him, "You are truly my disciples if you remain faithful to my teachings. Then you will know the truth, and the truth will set you free." 33, They answered him, "We are Abraham's descendants and have never been slaves of anyone. How can you say that we shall be set free?" 34, Jesus replied, "I tell you the truth, everyone who sins is a slave to sin. 35, Now a slave has no permanent place in the family, but a son belongs to it forever. 36, So if the Son sets you free, you will be free indeed." *"I"*, might be typing these words, but God said them! And that's the Truth! So why do we still struggle with sin and addictions? I believe that the Bible, God's Word, and the Eternal, absolute Truth, has all the answers we'll ever need in life. But if we're not using it daily, in search for those answers, and as our armor against spiritual warfare, we can't win the battle we're in. (Eph. 6:12-14) We need to be suited up daily in all of God's armor, and draw close to Him, (James 4:8), to be able to hear Him and His answers to our prayers and petitions. If we don't, we'll be led astray by the army of the enemy, the many false teachers in the world today, who are led by Satan, who wants to lead us directly to Hell if we give him the slightest opportunity!

It's our choice. We can continue on the path we're on, mired in our sin and addictions, or we can draw closer to God, (James 4:8), and accept His Word as the absolute Truth. Reading (2 Thessalonians 2:10-12 (NIV) may help us to make the right choice, to see and accept God's Word as the Absolute Truth. 10, "and all the ways that wickedness deceives those who are perishing. They perish because they refused to love the truth and so be saved. 11, For this reason God sends them a powerful delusion so that they will believe the lie 12 and so that all will be condemned who have not believed the truth but have delighted in wickedness".) We need to live out His Word in all areas of our lives. If we profess to be believers, we must begin to believe that His Word and His Promises are the Truth, whether we understand them or not.

I know of no one who understands the entire Bible, but many however, who claim too. Those who claim to know or understand it all, frequently turn out to be the false teachers who will lead us astray. God won't allow that to happen if He knows we're diligently seeking His Truth. We must all become like the Bereans in Acts 17:11, and search the scripture daily, first for wisdom, then to compare it with what we're being told by church leaders, to confirm that it lines up with God's Word. His Word is full of promises and guidance that will lead us in the right direction, and to the right answers if we're patient and seeking His will in our lives. One of the many promises for those of us struggling with addictions and other sin, is that we are "set Free" from the bondage to sin, and given the "power of the Holy Spirit" when we're Born Again. With these two free gifts alone, along with the Faith of a mustard seed, there is no reason for us to continue in our addictions. We should be Saved and Sober!

One area that many of us fall short in, because of decades, if not centuries of false teaching, is understanding that many of Gods promises are conditional. That we are obligated to do something for Him in return for His promise, or to receive it in the first place. Many of these promises require our obedience to His Will for us. Even our Salvation is contingent upon our repentance. In Acts 2:38, Peter replied, "Each of you must repent of your sins and turn to God, and be baptized in the name of Jesus Christ for the forgiveness of your sins. Then you will receive the gift of the Holy Spirit. The promise of being "set free" is also conditional, In John 8:31-32, Jesus says, "You are truly my disciples, *if* you *remain faithful to my teachings*. 32 And you will know the truth, and the truth will set you free." We will be set free, "***IF***" we remain Faithful to His teachings, which means we must be obedient.

We don't need a degree in rocket science or theology, to understand basic Biblical Truths. If we can read and understand the English language, and have the faith of "a Mustard seed," and believe God's Word is the absolute Truth, then we should realize that we're no longer "Powerless", and in bondage to addictions. That we've been "set free" and can claim the "victory" He promises us in 1 Cor. 15:57 and 1 John 5:4.

The Truth has been under attack since the Garden. Adam and Eve fell for Satan's lies then, and we're still falling for them today. The difference is, we have the ability to have a copy of His Word with us at all times, in many different translations and languages, in print, or on our laptop, or now even on our cell phone, wherever we are and whenever we want, we have instant access to His Word. Yet, many of us fail to use it at all, and wonder why "God's not answering" when we call out to Him in time of need. When we can't hear

God, it has nothing to do with our ears. (John 8:47) He speaks to us through our heart and Spirit, and if our heart is cold and hard towards Him, our fellowship and relationship with Him will never grow, and that's what He wants most from us. He created us for Fellowship and a relationship with Him! For us "to draw near to Him" (James 4:8), and build a close personal relationship with Him. He wants us to Love Him, as He Loves us! And as we begin to want to love Him, we'll begin to trust Him, to recognize His Truth, and to want to obey His commands.

    I believe that we, as the church today, because of years of false teachings, have a serious problem regarding our obedience to God. We have a "cultural problem", according to A.W. Tozer, who commented years ago, "A whole new generation of Christians has come up believing that it is possible to "accept" Christ, without forsaking the world". We're no longer getting solid Biblical Truth in Sunday's message. We're besieged with "new age, pop culture, feel good" messages that take precedence over the Truth. Sin is being tolerated in the church, if repentance is not being preached. "Behold, darkness shall cover the earth, and gross darkness the people". (Isaiah 60:2) "Where there is no vision, the people perish". (Prov. 29:18) There can be no vision in the dark! (Ps. 119:105) In "The need of the hour", by Oswald J. Smith, he says "This is true today…people on every side are in almost total darkness, so far as God's Salvation is concerned. Only here and there do we find a pulpit where the Gospel is preached, the new birth emphasized, Salvation made plain, and an Invitation given." I would ad that the message of Repentance has been forgotten as well, and many churches today seem to "assume" their entire congregation has repented and been saved. All for the sake of filling their auditoriums. (And bank accounts)? Our

Salvation is imperative to permanent addiction recovery.

Traditional, secular, 12-step addiction recovery programs are little less than cults. These programs hide in sheep's clothing, claiming to have Christian roots and founders. But they're wolves seeking to devour their members. They have no interest in spreading The Gospel and sharing the Good News to the lost and hurting millions of addicts that attend their meetings worldwide. The Good News that Jesus Christ can "set them free" from the bondage of their addictions. Neither is God's Word, His Son, Jesus Christ, Salvation, personal prayer, The Holy Spirit, or "setting the captives free," even allowed to be mentioned or discussed in their meetings. They actually teach that one can never be free from addiction, that you must "keep coming back, it works," is a common expression ending all meetings. Another common and hopeless expression heard at all meetings is "once a drunk, always a drunk"! Only a cult could claim to be a Christian program, and deny Christ! Titus 1:16, "Such people claim they know God, but they deny him by the way they live. They are detestable and disobedient, worthless for doing anything good."

As long as these traditional, secular, 12-step addiction recovery programs exist in a worldly environment, they're of little consequence to the Christian struggling with addictions. The Christian is not obligated to participate in a secular program, although there has never been many alternative choices for us, and God doesn't allow it according to scripture, "Do not participate in the unfruitful works of darkness, but instead even expose them." (Ephesians 5:11-12) Also if an AA meeting claimed to be a Christian program and referred to you as a brother, this scripture might apply to the situation, 1 Cor. 5:11, "But now I am writing you that you must not associate with anyone who calls himself a brother but is sexually immoral or greedy, an idolater or a slanderer, a drunkard or a swindler. With such a man do not even eat."…or… 2 Cor. 6:14, "Do not be yoked together with unbelievers. For what do righteousness and wickedness have in common? Or what fellowship can light have with darkness?" I've been in this exact situation a number of times in AA meetings where men "profess" to be "brothers" in the Lord, yet their behavior would indicate otherwise. Any program or organization that claims to be Christian, yet denies Christ Crucified and the Cross, is a *"CULT"!* My brothers and sisters in Christ should avoid participating in these programs at all costs, as the leaders are led by satan, who will stop at nothing to deceive you and lead you straight to Hell! The three scriptures above should be more than enough of God's Word to convince you to the danger of exposing yourself to worldly evil.

Again, as long as these traditional, secular, 12-step addiction recovery programs exist in a worldly environment, such as your local neighborhood AA meeting, they're of little consequence to the Christian struggling with addictions. What concerns me with a heavy heart is the recent infiltration and permeation of traditional, secular, 12-step addiction recovery programs into thousands of Christian churches around the world during the past decade or so. They've saturated the Christian Church addiction recovery groups with their false teachings and blasphemy, and even brainwashed its members. A few years ago while leading one of these meetings in a large mega-church, a member who had been attending our meetings for a year or so, stated that he wasn't sure if he believed AA's Big Book or the Bible. This shows the power the devil can have on individuals who have been led astray by cults like AA. It confounds me to try to understand how a church leader or pastor can be so easily deceived, and not recognize the clear and obvious shortcomings and blasphemy exhorted throughout these secular 12-step addiction recovery programs. How can anyone in Christian leadership roles, familiar with the words of Jesus in Acts 1:8, justify telling a born again believer that he or she is powerless, which are the instructions in step #1. And the list of other blasphemy in these programs is endless.

    Therein, I believe lies part of the answer to the question, "Why do Christians struggle with addictions and other sin?" If our churches aren't teaching the Truth, Christians in addiction recovery, aren't hearing the Truth, and the most vulnerable members in the congregation need to hear the Truth to be Set Free. They need all of the Truth, without any sugar-coating, or feel-good addendums or watered-down Gospel. Alcoholics and addicts who have been in recovery for awhile are extremely vulnerable, broken, tired and worn out folks who will not tolerate being lied to, or pandered. They need to hear the Truth, no matter how painful it might be. Most alcoholics and addicts have already suffered more pain than is imaginable, and would find Gods Truth, delivered in a straightforward way, comforting when realizing it's the only way for them to be set free from the pain and destruction they've been through. They need a form of "hard Love," along with hugs, compassion, and understanding. A difficult task indeed for the wisest Christian counselor, and one that will never be successful if started with false teaching. I have much to say in future chapters regarding the multitudes of alcoholics and addicts who drop out of recovery because they've been let down by churches and programs that try to teach them a bunch of nonsense and lies.

    It will take God's "light" to break through this darkness, (John 8:12), the darkness mentioned above in Isaiah 60:2, which is covering the earth and it's people today! The purpose of this book is to expose the lies, and reveal the Truth through the light of God's Word. To show the captives in bondage to addictions, that they've already been "set free" if they're Born Again, and that they have the "power" (Acts 1:8), to claim the "Victory" over their bondage! (1 Cor. 15:57, 1 John 5:4) Again, John 8:31-36 promises it! Let's not turn down this free gift, or allow the enemy to deceive us into believing that this promise is not the Truth. All of God's Word is the Truth! If we're going to follow any "name-it-and-claim-it" teachings, let's name the above scriptures our "Hope", and "claim it" as a promise from God to us personally to stand on!

This free gift of freedom and victory was won for us on the Cross! By not claiming it, we're calling God a liar, and denying His Truth and Love for us, ultimately denying Him! Wake up Church! Wake up all of you afflicted with addictions and other sin! Let's get our heads out of the sand, take a deep breath, and allow some oxygen into our brains. It's time to turn from the evil, wicked ways of the world. Turn off the TV's and the internet, hang up the telephone, stay away from Starbucks, tear up your credit cards if you can't control them, and boycott the shopping centers, get off the golf courses and race tracks, and out of the stadiums, restaurants, and especially the bars and clubs! Let's start seeking and studying God's Word prayerfully and diligently, fellowship with one another, seeking Revelation of the Truth, and start serving God, not the world! Knowing, understanding, and accepting God's Truth is vital to our recovery and our Salvation!

Because of decades of false teaching in many churches, many who profess Christ as their Savior, aren't convinced that all of His Word is the Truth. They want to pick and choose what fits their lifestyle. Until we begin to live our lives according to His Word, we'll miss out on many of His Blessings. Possibly even our Salvation. We must understand a Truth that's rarely shared any more, is that most of Gods promises are conditional, and require our obedience and Faith. For God is the Truth, (John 14:6), and if we choose not to believe that, then how can we believe any of His Word and promises, including John 3:3, which says we need to be "Born Again" to be Saved. Or Acts 3:19 and 26:20, that tells us to ***repent and turn to God,*** and be Saved. We don't get to pick and choose what we want to believe, and dismiss what we don't. We don't get to call ourselves "Christians" without forsaking the world, (repenting), and realizing that "all" of God's Word is the Truth, and exercising our Faith! God knows the difference between a confession of the lips, and a confession of the Heart.

    The sooner we recognize our deadly state of denial, not just of our addictions and sin, but also of the promises God has made to us in His Word, the sooner we'll be "set free" from our bondage to addictions and other sin! God miraculously heals the sick, and sets captives free from their bondage, every second of every minute of every day, surrender now to Him, and be the next miracle! If the Truth and being born again is necessary for our Salvation, it's certainly necessary for our recovery from addictions! The Scripture is perfectly clear, be Born Again, believe God's Word is the Truth, Trust Him through Faith, be Set Free, and be **"SAVED and SOBER!"**

CHAPTER 6

Our Addictions Are Habitual Sin

John 5:14,
Afterward Jesus findeth him in the temple, and said unto him, Behold, thou art made whole: sin no more, lest a worse thing come unto thee. John 8:11, She said, No man, Lord. And Jesus said unto her, Neither do I condemn thee: go, and sin no more.
1 Cor. 15:57
"But thanks be to God! He gives us the victory through our Lord Jesus Christ."

Hebrews 10:26-27 NIV,
If we deliberately keep on sinning after we have received the knowledge of the truth, no sacrifice for sins is left, 27 but only a fearful expectation of judgment and of raging fire that will consume the enemies of God.

    Satan knows exactly which buttons to push to keep us defeated and wallowing in the chaos, pain, and misery of our addictions and sin. Once he's established a foothold in our life, our denial will keep us blinded to the truth, and we'll become experts at finding excuses to defend our actions. The longer we spend fighting addictions, the higher the wall of denial becomes, and as we continue to master the tricks of deception, and become great chameleons with all those around us, the harder it becomes to break through the wall of denial.
    Millions of Christians today have been mislead into believing that the words in 1 John 1:8-10 are a

license to sin. The first words out of their mouths in defense, and to justify their sinful behavior, is usually, "you're judging me, we're all sinners." Another favorite excuse is taking Romans 7:14-20 out of context and justifying their sinful behavior with it. Yes, we're all sinners and will fail when we are weak. When we do, we need to fall to our knees in sorrow, and with a broken heart, repent and seek God's forgiveness, not shrug our shoulders and say, "oh well, we're all sinners, no big deal." That attitude is what makes our sin willful, and will not be forgiven according to Hebrews 10:26-27, or Isaiah 57:17, "I was enraged by their sinful greed; I punished them, and hid my face in anger, yet they kept on in their willful ways." Or Jesus words in Luke 16:15 KJV, And he said unto them, "Ye are they which justify yourselves before men; but God knoweth your hearts: for that which is highly esteemed among men is abomination in the sight of God." Again, yes we're all sinners and will fail when we are weak, but we cannot make excuses for it when we do.

The temptation to sin, no matter what our addiction might be, is overwhelming until we learn to completely trust God, and understand His Word. Trusting God is a matter of how much Faith we have and display, or put into practice. It is one thing to *claim* we have great Faith, and another thing to display it, or show it through our actions. Faith is a measure of our dependence on God in all areas of our lives. When we're born again, some of us surrender completely, and immediately, and are filled with great Faith, trusting God completely in all things and areas of our lives. Others tend to only let go of bits and pieces of our old selves, wanting to hold onto certain cherished worldly sin. (2 Tim. 2:22) speaks to this issue. Matthew 16:8 speaks to the issue of "Ye of little Faith," while Matthew 15:28 speaks to the opposing issue in "Woman, you have great faith! Your request is granted." The choice as always is ours, and the longer we take to choose to give "My Utmost for His Highest," the longer it will take to hear His words, "Your request is granted." The longer it will take to conquer the temptation to sin, to end addictions, to be set free, and to be Saved and Sober!

Charles Stanley had this to say about ending habitual sin. "Satan looks for weak spots in a believer's life where he can set up a stronghold. Once his fortress is established, he knows that the person will justify it, defend it, and keep adding bricks to it, one sin at a time. The appeal can be so strong that we return to a habitual sin even after confessing before God. Satan whispers, "One more time won't hurt," and we fall to temptation again.

Just as in medieval times when armies warred over high rock fortresses, a sin stronghold is usually the ground for a skirmish. We might expect the fight to be primarily between God and Satan, but that's not the case—the Lord can knock down the Devil's walls instantly. Instead, the struggle goes on within our spirit: Do we want God to break our habit or not? Giving up habitual sin is hard. The sinner finds comfort, pleasure, and or satisfaction in the practice. Hot on the heels of those emotions, however, are guilt, shame, and despair, which drive a person to plead for help. But holy God cannot cleanse unrighteousness until people genuinely repent. True repentance means that a believer sees a sin for the wickedness that it is and turns his back on it. And we turn away as often as it takes—one time, a hundred times, or every single day for the rest of our lives.

According to Charles Stanley, "Just thinking about giving up a sinful habit brings some people to the brink of despair. They want to be free of a stronghold, but the thought of resisting temptation makes them feel weak. Here is good news: the Holy

Spirit's power is enough to enable any believer to walk away. That includes you."

Repentance is vital to our addiction recovery, to being set free from the bondage of all sin, just as vital as it is to our Salvation. Herein lies perhaps the biggest battle in this Spiritual warfare. Repentance is turning from our sin. No matter how much Faith we have, no matter how badly we want to turn from our addictions, satan doesn't want to let go of us! His job is to keep you locked up, messed up, feeling hopeless, helpless, broken, useless, and alone. He's been doing this for a long time, and is very good at it. God, on the other hand, is much better at what He does. He offers you His Armor, (Eph. 6:10-12), "Finally, be strong in the Lord and in his mighty power. 11, Put on the full armor of God so that you can take your stand against the devil's schemes. 12, For our struggle is not against flesh and blood, but against the rulers, against the authorities, against the powers of this dark world and against the spiritual forces of evil in the heavenly realms." You have Gods Word, the sword of the Spirit, and if you use it you will defeat the enemy, if you don't use it he will defeat you. Note that I said, "***IF***" you use it, or don't. It's not just a matter of reading it, or memorizing your favorite passages, but it's crucial to our Salvation *and* our addiction recovery, to apply His Word in our daily life, in everything we do. It's a very simple Truth my friend, and as I say over and over again, it's your choice, no one else can make it for you, and the longer it takes you to accept this simple truth, the longer you'll stay in the bondage to your addictions and sin.

While Gods Word, the Truth, may be relatively simple to understand, there is nothing simple about defeating the enemy! There's still more required of us than repenting, showing Faith, and putting on the armor of God, to defeat the enemy and to be set free, to conquer the battle over our habitual sin. We must also develop as part of our relationship with God, a close personal level of communication with Him. We must develop a new and routine habit of Prayer. Pray without ceasing, (1 Thessalonians 5:16-18) needs to become the #1 priority in our lives. It's the only way we can share with God our feelings, questions, and needs, as well as a way to praise Him for all that He does for us. It's also the only way for us to hear His answers and directions for our guidance. I often ask Christians who are struggling with trials, and complaining that their prayers aren't seemingly being answered, "Are your knees bleeding"? Meaning, are they diligently "praying without ceasing," and in Faith. (James 5:15) Are you praying from your closet, (Matthew 6:6), or from a mountaintop, (Luke 6:12), where it's quiet, and you can hear yourself think without the loud noises and distractions of the world. You also need peace and quiet and serenity to be able to hear Gods voice. Luke 21:36 says, "Watch ye therefore, and pray always, that ye may be accounted worthy to escape all these things that shall come to pass, and to stand before the Son of man." Psalm 120:1, "I call on the Lord in my distress, and he answers me."

    Finally, another important element of winning our battles, defeating the enemy, and being set free from our bondage to addictions, is being obedient to God's Will. Most of the promises God has made to us are conditional, and require something from us in return. For example "to be set free," we see in John 8:31 that He says, "*If*... you hold to my teaching,…we will be set free. In Deuteronomy 28:1-2 NIV , we read, "*If* ... you fully obey the Lord your God and carefully follow all his commands I give you today, the Lord your God will set you high above all the nations on earth. All these blessings will come upon you and accompany you *if*... you obey the Lord your God." Even our Salvation is conditional upon our obedience according to, 1 Corinthians 15:2, "By this gospel you are saved, *if*...you hold firmly to the word I preached to you. Otherwise, you have believed in vain." How much simpler can Gods Word be? As long as we fail to follow His instructions, we will fail to receive His Blessings. We will remain in the bondage of our addictions, and continue to suffer the consequences of them.

In summary, even being born again, being set free from our addictions is not promised to us without conditions we must follow. Picking up our Cross and following Christ is definitely a different journey for each of us, depending upon Gods specific and perfect plan He has for our lives. I've met many Christians over the years who were set free from their addictions almost immediately after surrendering their lives to Christ. I've met many others who struggled with their addictions for years, one relapse after another, and usually due to a lack of Faith and or obedience, or for other reasons that only God knows. He may decide that some of us need more "refining" to be brought into further submission to obedience and Faith. Only He knows when we've been refined enough according to His plan for us. I've met still many other people who, for whatever reason, spend their entire lives refusing to be obedient to Gods will for them and eventually burn out and turn their backs on God. He will not force us to obey Him. It is only by our Faith and obedience which comes from our Love for Him, that we can defeat the enemy, and become victorious over our addictions. The longer it takes us to give up our worldly ego and pride and selfishness, the more time in the fire we'll be required to spend to learn and accept God's Truth. Then, and only then, can we be "set free" from habitual sin.

We have the choice and free will to repent and

turn to, and surrender our lives and wills over to The Almighty God, and His Son Jesus Christ, and to be "set free", and be **"SAVED and SOBER"!**

CHAPTER 7

Truth or Consequences

Ezekiel 23:35 (KJV)
"Therefore this is what the Sovereign Lord says: Since you have forgotten me and turned your back on me, you must bear the consequences of your lewdness and prostitution."

1 Corinthians 11:29-32 (The Message)
"If you give no thought (or worse, don't care) about the broken body of the Master when you eat and drink, you're running the risk of serious consequences. That's why so many of you even now are listless and sick, and others have gone to an early grave. If we get this straight now, we won't have to be straightened out later on. Better to be confronted by the Master now than to face a fiery confrontation later."

Eternal Death in the pit of hell is the number one consequence of not accepting and believing Gods Truth! "The more men suppress the Truth of God, which they know, the more futile, even senseless, they become in their thinking." - John R.W. Scott (1921-).

I concur with author Patrick Morley, in his book "Man in The Mirror," not only do I agree with him, but I would strongly recommend to anyone reading this material, to take the time to read his book in full, and if you already have, read it again. It will help you understand the message I'm trying to reveal in my writings about the failure of the Church in regards to addiction recovery. Mr. Morley states in chapter 3, that we, as the church today, have a "cultural problem." We're either "Cultural Christians or Biblical Christians. And each of us fits into one of these four groups he defines as, the non-Christian, (Luke 8:12), the Cultural Christian type "C," (Luke 8:13), the Cultural Christian type "D," (Luke 8:14), and the Biblical Christian, (Luke 8:15) I believe "the head of the nail has been smashed to smithereens," when Mr. Morley suggests that many people believe "that all they need to do is 'pray a prayer' and they will be saved-born again. Everyone, it seems has 'prayed a prayer!' Prayer doesn't save; *Faith* saves!"

As A.W. Tozer quoted years ago, "A whole new generation of Christians has come up believing that it is possible to "accept" Christ, without forsaking the world!" We're no longer getting solid Biblical Truth in Sunday's message. Instead, we're overwhelmed with "new age, pop culture, feel good, watered down and sugar-coated" messages that take precedence over the Truth. I believe, "*Sin* is being tolerated, if *repentance* is not being preached." "Behold, darkness shall cover the earth, and gross darkness the people." (Isaiah 60:2) "Where there is no vision, the people perish." (Prov. 29:18) There can be no vision in the dark! (Ps. 119:105) In "The Need of the Hour", by Oswald J. Smith, he says "This is true today…people on every side are in almost total darkness, so far as Gods Salvation is concerned. Only here and there do we find a pulpit where the *Gospel* is preached, the *new birth* emphasized, *Salvation* made plain, and an *invitation* given." *I* would add also, that the message of *Repentance* has been forgotten as well, and that many churches today seem to *assume* their entire congregation has repented and been saved. When, in fact, all they've done is "prayed a simple prayer" without repenting or having any Faith! Are these churches guilty of making this *assumption* simply for the sake of filling their auditoriums, (and bank accounts)? Knowing that no one wants to accept the *Truth*, that they have to give up their much adored sin to be saved! Repentance is vital to our Salvation *and* our addiction recovery. (Acts 3:19, 17:30, 26:20, Ezekiel 18:30, 32, Matthew 3:2, 2 Cor. 12:21, 2 Pet. 3:9, Rev. 3:3)

Now let's jump ahead to *why* they're "praying this prayer without faith," or claiming Salvation without repenting, or thinking that they must be Christians, simply "because they grew up going to a church with their parents every Sunday, listening to "False teachings by false teachers." (Acts 15:24, 2 Corinthians 11:4, Galatians 1:7, Galatians 2:4, 2 Peter 2, Jude 1:3-25) It's been going on since the *Garden*, and is far more prevalent today than ever before! False teaching is either teaching or proclaiming a lie, or *avoiding to teach* the Truth at all. Whether deceitfully and intentionally, or unintentionally out of ignorance, there is no excuse for it. Neither is there any excuse to be a victim, *if* we're being like the Bereans in Acts 17:11. "Now the Berean Jews were of more noble character than those in Thessalonica, for they received the message with great eagerness and examined the Scriptures every day to see if what Paul said was true."

False teaching will lead lost souls to Hell! False teaching leads to the creation and growth of the many cults and sects and "lukewarm" (Rev. 3:16) churches that are rampantly spreading around the world today. Paul clearly detested false teachers in (Gal. 1:8-9), when he suggests that they be "eternally condemned" (NIV). We should follow Paul's lead today when confronted by, or exposed to false teachers, or their *teachings.* If we've survived infancy as a Christian, and grown into mature Christians, (Heb. 5:11-13), It's our duty as Christ's servants, to expose these lies when God has revealed them to us! My personal translation, ("in the vernacular") of (Gal. 1:8-9), when I see my brothers and sisters in Christ being deliberately and or recklessly misled through false teachings, "eternally condemned" means "may they, (the false teachers) "rot in hell"!

Scripture used *"Out of Context,"* is perhaps one of the leading causes for *"misleading* believers". We see scripture everyday being used out of context to make a point of one thing or another, having absolutely no bearing on the subject or topic at hand. Unless we're grounded personally and individually in God's Holy Word, and acting as the Bereans did in (Acts 17:11), we're open to the enemies deception. While it may not affect our Salvation, It will surely affect our daily lives in addiction recovery. And if we're Christians struggling with addictions, we need to hear The Truth, and "***nothing*** *but the Truth"!* If we're Christians in recovery, sugar-coated, watered down, half truths will only keep us in our addictions. Hearing messages with scripture being used out of context is the least of our problems. We need to be aware of the pure Heresy and Blasphemy that's slithering its way into our churches today that are using the traditional secular 12-step programs such as AA, to counsel their members struggling with addictions.

The Truth has been under attack since the garden. Adam and Eve fell for Satan's lies then, and *we're* still falling for them today. The difference is, *we* have the ability to have a copy of His Word with us at all times, in many different translations and languages, in print, or on our laptop and now even on our cell phones, wherever we are. All we need to do is to be like the Bereans, (Act 17:11) and search the scripture daily to make sure what we're being taught is the Truth. Yet many of us fail to use these resources at all, and then wonder why "God's not answering" when we call out in time of need. (Isa.

58:9) We need to believe the Bible, God's written Word, and the Eternal, Absolute Truth, has all the answers we'll ever need in life. (2 Tim. 3:15-17) But if we're not using it daily, in search for those answers, and as our sword, (Eph. 6:17) against spiritual warfare, (Eph. 6:11) we can't win the battle with Satan for our souls. We need to be suited up daily in all of God's armor, and draw close to Him, (James 4:8), to be able to hear Him, (Rev. 2:7) and His answers to our prayers and petitions and his instructions for our lives. This is how we get to know and understand our living God and His Divine plan for our lives. If we don't, we'll be led astray by the army of the enemy, the many false teachers in the world today, who are led by Satan, who wants to lead us directly to Hell if we give him the slightest opportunity! (2 Pet. 2:1-22, 2 Tim. 3:13, 4:3-4) *(this is **must** read scripture!)*

One consequence of not knowing or recognizing the Truth is not being able to *hear* God. When we can't hear God, it has nothing to do with our *ears*. (John 8:47) He speaks to us through our heart, and if it's cold and hard towards Him, our relationship with Him will never grow, which is what He wants most from us. He created us for fellowship with Him! For us "to draw *near* to Him" (James 4:8), and build a close personal relationship with Him. He wants us to Love Him as much as He Loves us! And when we begin to *want* to Love Him, we'll begin to *hear* Him and to trust Him, to recognize His Truth, and to *want* to obey His commands. Then we'll begin receiving His blessings. We'll begin to recognize His working in our lives, and to understand His will and purpose for our lives.

Another consequence of not accepting and believing Gods Truth, is we'll miss out on His blessings for us. (Rev. 1:3, Jer. 17:7, Deut. 28:2) When we trust in the truth of God's Word, we begin to receive His blessings. If we don't "give our utmost for His highest", (Oswald Chambers, 1/1), we should expect less than *His Utmost* for us! We don't give Him our utmost, because we don't fully trust Him, and we can't fully trust Him until we get to know Him personally, and fully develop our faith in Him.

The Truths #1 enemy, besides Satan, is man's lies and philosophy. (Col. 2:8) "See to it that no one takes you captive through hollow and deceptive philosophy, which depends on human tradition and the basic principles of this world rather than on Christ."(NIV) I suggest we pray, meditate, and absorb this verse as if it were our "last supper." (Heb. 5:12-14) We need to recognize that the enemies been devouring the Church recently with false teaching. This is *not* a news flash, but the enemy is having a field day today with our many new modern advanced technological media devises which allow his lies to be spread around the world in seconds at the click of a mouse! As the Truth is being watered down, and replaced with lies and heresy, many souls are being lost to satan and *his* addictions!

In addiction recovery, the subject of truth or consequences is a very serious topic. The Truth can mean Eternal Life, while the consequence can mean Eternal death. Life or death? It would seem to be an easy decision, yet many seem to make choices that will lead to death. Why? Man, without God in his life, has no purpose in life. The secular world view and philosophy is that we are merely "dust in the wind." We have no purpose, meaning, or reason to live. Consequently, making critical choices regarding eternity, or that could ultimately lead to relapse, and worse, death, are easier to make.

Having *Purpose* in life, is one of the most fundamental *Truths* there is. God created us for, and with a purpose. Individually, He has a uniquely specific purpose and plan for each of our lives. He predestined us, and wants us all to hear and answer His call. In addiction recovery, if we haven't found our purpose in life, we're unlikely to find lasting, Eternal recovery. An occasional glimpse of temporary sobriety is possible, but permanent, Eternal, victory over our addictions is not likely. Until we've committed our lives and wills to Christ, we'll not discover our "true" purpose in life. We may have spent most of our lives thinking we were supposed to be doing "this or that", only to discover Christ, and the Truth, and the reality that He had no such plan for you. Simultaneously, you'll discover He never intended for you to be addicted to drugs, alcohol, or any other sin. You'll discover His promise to "set you free." (John 8:31-36) *And,* if you recognize and accept that promise as His absolute Truth, you'll claim it, and "be free indeed"! You'll be "recovered", not "*in recovery*" for the rest of your life. You'll be **"_Saved and Sober_",** all in **"_one_"** simple step! John 3:3 Please, my friends, take this simple step, trust God and His Truth, repent, and turn from the evil ways of this world that wants to keep you in the bondage of your addictions, repent, and turn to God! (Acts 3:19)

"TRUTH OR CONSEQUENCES"?

Accepting or denying the Truth is always a choice that each and every one of us needs to make someday. Regardless of the choice or the circumstance, the consequences are inevitable. Whether it's a major life changing choice, or the decision to pick up a bottle of poison and drink it, or have an affair with our neighbor, most of us already know the correct choice we should make, we've all been taught the difference between right and wrong, but sit in denial year after year, suffering the consequences of the bad choices we make. In addiction recovery, this is known as the insanity of making the same decisions over and over again, expecting different results. Most of us never give a moment's thought to the consequences until they become hindsight. The following scripture applies mostly to the biggest choice a man will ever face, which ultimately will affect every other choice he will ever make. The choice of accepting God and His Son, Jesus Christ, of repenting and following Him, trusting and obeying Him, is the most important decision a man will ever make in his life. All other choices in life are relevant to this one. We can do nothing without Him, and *all* things with Him!

THE TRUTH,...

Psalm 25:5 NIV "guide me in your ***truth*** and teach me, for you are God my Savior, and my hope is in you all day long."

Psalm 43:3 "Send forth your light and your ***truth***, let them guide me; let them bring me to your holy mountain, to the place where you dwell."

John 4:23 "Yet a time is coming and has now come when the true worshipers will worship the Father in spirit and ***truth***, for they are the kind of worshipers the Father seeks."

John 8:32 "Then you will know the ***truth***, and the ***truth*** will set you free."

John 14:6 Jesus answered, "I am the way and the ***truth*** and the life. No one comes to the Father except through me."

John 17:17 "Sanctify them by the ***truth***; your word is ***truth***."

1 Timothy 2:3-5 3, "This is good, and pleases God our Savior, 4, who wants all men to be saved and to come to a knowledge of the *"**truth**."* 5, For there is one God and one mediator between God and men, the man Christ Jesus,"

1 John 1:6 "If we claim to have fellowship with him yet walk in the darkness, we lie and do not live

by the _"truth."_

OR THE CONSEQUENCES,...
The consequences are either Blessings or curses.

The Blessing of Eternal Life is the Ultimate **_consequence_** of accepting and believing God's **_Truth!_**

The curse of Eternal death is the Ultimate **_consequence_** of **_not_** accepting and believing God's **_Truth!_**

The Blessings,...

Psalm 65:4 "**_Blessed_** are those you choose and bring near to live in your courts! We are filled with the good things of your house, of your holy temple."

Psalm 84:12 "O Lord Almighty, **_blessed_** is the man who trusts in you."

Jeremiah 17:7 "But **_blessed_** is the man who trusts in the Lord, whose confidence is in him.

Deuteronomy 28:1-2 "If you fully obey the Lord your God and carefully follow all his commands I give you today, the Lord your God will set you high above all the nations on earth. All these **_blessings_** will come upon you and accompany you if you obey the Lord your God:

John 8:31-32, To the Jews who had believed him, Jesus said, "If you hold to my teaching, you are really my disciples. Then you will know the **_truth_**, and the **_truth_** will set you free."

1 Corinthians 13:6 "Love does not delight in evil but rejoices with the **_truth_**."

Ephesians 1:13 "And you also were included in Christ when you heard the word of **_truth_**, the gospel of your salvation. Having believed, you were marked in him with a seal, the promised Holy

Spirit,"

Colossians 1:5-6, "The faith and love that spring from the hope that is stored up for you in heaven and that you have already heard about in the word of "***truth***," the gospel 6, That has come to you. All over the world this gospel is bearing fruit and growing, just as it has been doing among you since the day you heard it and understood God's grace in all its truth."

The Curses,…or the consequences,…

Proverbs 22:3 "A prudent person foresees danger and takes precautions. The simpleton goes blindly on and suffers the ***consequences***."

Ezekiel 23:35, "Therefore this is what the Sovereign Lord says: Since you have forgotten me and turned your back on me, you must bear the ***consequences*** of your lewdness and prostitution."

Ezekiel 23:49, "You will suffer the penalty for your lewdness and bear the ***consequences*** of your sins of idolatry. Then you will know that I am the Sovereign Lord."

1 Corinthians 11:29-32 The Message,

"If you give no thought (or worse, don't care) about the broken body of the Master when you eat and drink, you're running the risk of serious ***consequences***. That's why so many of you even now are listless and sick, and others have gone to an early grave. If we get this straight now, we won't have to be straightened out later on. Better to be confronted by the Master now than to face a fiery confrontation later."

Jeremiah 7:28 Therefore say to them, "This is the nation that has not obeyed the LORD its God or responded to correction. ***Truth*** has perished; it has vanished from their lips."

Jeremiah 9:3 "They make ready their tongue like a bow, to shoot lies; it is not by ***Truth*** that they triumph in the land. They go from one sin to another; they do not acknowledge me," declares the LORD.

Jeremiah 11:3 "Tell them that this is what the Lord, the God of Israel, says: "***Cursed*** is the man who does not obey the terms of this covenant—

Jeremiah 17:5 "This is what the Lord says: "***Cursed*** is the one who trusts in man, who depends on flesh for his strength and whose heart turns away from the Lord."

Malachi 2:2 "If you do not listen, and if you do not set your heart to honor my name," says the Lord Almighty, "I will send a ***curse*** upon you, and I will ***curse*** your blessings. Yes, I have already ***cursed*** them, because you have not set your heart to honor me."

1 Corinthians 16:22, "If anyone does not love the Lord—a ***curse*** be on him. Come, O Lord!"

The Truth,...

Romans 1:18-19, "The wrath of God is being revealed from heaven against all the godlessness and wickedness of men who suppress the ***truth*** by their wickedness, 19: since what may be known about God is plain to them, because God has made it plain to them."

Romans 2:8, "But for those who are self-seeking and who reject the ***truth*** and follow evil, there will be wrath and anger."

2 Thessalonians 2:10, "and in every sort of evil that deceives those who are perishing. They perish because they refused to love the ***truth*** and so be saved."

2 Thessalonians 2:12; "and so that all will be condemned who have not believed the ***truth*** but have delighted in wickedness."

2 Timothy 3:7-8 "Always learning but never able to acknowledge the ***truth***. "

Just as Jannes and Jambres opposed Moses, so

also these men oppose the ***truth***—men of depraved minds, who, as far as the faith is concerned, are rejected."

2 Timothy 4:4, "They will turn their ears away from the ***truth*** and turn aside to myths."

Hebrews 10:26 "If we deliberately keep on sinning after we have received the knowledge of the ***truth***, no sacrifice for sins is left,

1 John 1:6 "If we claim to have fellowship with him yet walk in the darkness, we lie and do not live by the ***truth***."

1 John 2:4 "The man who says, "I know him," but does not do what he commands is a liar, and the ***truth*** is not in him."

What then shall we choose, The Truth or The Consequences? We have the same choice today that we've had since the beginning of time in the garden. Just as God gave Adam and Eve directions to follow, and a choice to do so, or not to do so, today, we also have directions to follow, and the free choice to do so or not. We have the choice to repent and turn to, and surrender our lives and wills over to The Almighty God, and His Son Jesus Christ, and to be "set free", and be **"SAVED and SOBER"**!

CHAPTER 8

Denial

The devils most lethal weapon against an Addict

Jeremiah 9:5
"Friend deceives friend, and no one speaks the truth. They have taught their tongues to lie; they weary themselves with sinning". Proverbs 14:8 NLT, "The prudent understand where they are going, but fools deceive themselves."

Denial is what keeps a person trapped in their addictions. Sometimes for years, and even decades. Many never see through the veil of deception, and end up spending their entire lives stuck in the bondage of addictions. The simplest definition of denial is when a person asserts that a statement or allegation against them is not true, or a person's defense mechanism, that when a person is faced with a fact that is too painful to admit and accept, so denies and rejects it instead, insisting that it is not true despite what may be overwhelming evidence to the contrary. Or they might minimize it and deny its seriousness (a combination of denial and rationalization). Another very common excuse and demeanor is often expressed in the comment, "It's my life, I'll do what I want with it, and I'm not hurting anyone but myself." Showing total disregard for everyone around them. Christians will build on this theme by adding, "we're all sinners, who are you to judge me?" Pride and ignorance is always at the root of denial.

Blaming someone else or some circumstance for their problems is always the first line of defense for an alcoholic or an addict. They're always the victim, never the perpetrator. They have a million excuses why it's never their fault. They never accept the responsibility that it was their *choice* to take their first drink or drug, or the next one, or the hundredth, or the thousandth, until they reach the point that denial is no longer an option. Some people never reach this point, and die addicted and in denial of the truth and reality of their problem. Everyone else reaches this point of acceptance that they have a problem at different stages of their addictions. Many others reach it over and over again, as they continuously relapse. Many have tried a number of different 12-step programs and recovery facilities, to no avail.

Today we see tens of thousands of men and women spending perhaps billions of dollars a year of their own money, as well as our tax dollars and insurance company's money, on rehab programs that can cost up to $1000.00 a day! As more and more of the rich and famous fall deeper into addictions, resulting eventually into joining the ranks of the homeless in the alleys of the slums through-out America, there's a new fad growing, a whole new meaning and perspective to being "a drunk or an addict. If you're rich, money can buy you a 30 day stay at the "Hilton Rehab Spa and Beachfront Country Club," whether you've stepped out of denial or not. The CEO of this facility doesn't care if you're in denial or not, his only interest in you is your bank account. More than likely if your pockets are deep enough, he'd ***prefer*** that you're still in denial. Many of these facilities' owners have themselves, done time in AA meetings where one of many motto's is "keep coming back, it works." If these Recovery Country Clubs can keep the same people coming back, they can save a great deal of money on promotion and marketing for new clients.

If you're one of these rich and famous celebrities, and don't see this as truth and reality, you probably should write them a check for a reservation for another stay within the next 180 days. For almost everyone else, the only option they have for treatment is an AA meeting. Or, if you're lucky there might be a Christ centered, Gospel teaching, addiction recovery program somewhere nearby, that can lead them to the Truth, that Christ can "set us free." (John 8:31-36) A big problem is that even if you lived across the street from the best Christian addiction recovery program in the world, many people who call themselves Christians, are in denial of His Word being the Truth. If their denial is being fed by pride and they're unwilling to admit that they have a problem, no matter what or how destructive that problem might be, the only hope that person has is the Grace of God. I've become quite cynical during the past 10 years of the addiction recovery system as a whole, but especially in Churches that have allowed secular programs to council there members. I've watched thousands of men and women crawl in and out of meetings and programs, rehab facilities, hospitals, jails and prisons, over and over again, with the same puke stained shirts and shoes, pleading for help, and the only answer they ever hear is, "do the 12-steps." My frustration is not with the denial that people show towards their addictions, which is almost a natural psychological reaction, but with the Christian community that denies Christ's promises and Power, which they would receive when they're born again and receive the Holy Spirit. (John 3:3, and Acts 1:8) To deny His Word, is denying Him, thus denying their Salvation. To show doubt, is a lack of Faith, and satan loves destroying a

Christians Faith, which turns them from God. (Titus 1:16)

The proliferation of false teachings throughout the world today, is feeding millions of lost souls the idea that they can be Saved as easily as buying a hamburger at a fast food drive through! There is nothing more to it than a quick "repeat after me" vow by a church leader who then proclaims you're "saved"! No mention of repentance, obedience, or Faith, just "tithe, and name your blessing and claim it"! These lies have been, and will continue to lead millions of lost souls, who believe they've been saved, straight to hell! And millions of these lost souls who are unfortunate enough to be struggling with addictions, will never overcome them until they discover the Gospel Truth and surrender to it. Prayerfully, this book will help clear up some of those lies, and lead many not only to recovery, but to Salvation.

Addiction is still exactly the same perilous, dead-end tragedy that it was 100 years ago, all that's changed is the nature of the victims, the drugs of choice, and the society in which we exist. Denial is still the leading reason why people spend so much time in their addictions. The world is a completely different planet than what it was a mere century ago. The Model T has been replaced with computerized missiles on 4 wheels. The message that would take a month to deliver across the world, now takes a split second at the click of a "mouse." We no longer have to chop wood to cook with, instead we "microwave" a frozen pizza or TV dinner. Instead of the Morse code on the telegraph to communicate with one another, we now have cell phones. The only way for air travel used to be in a blimp, recently, it's been noted that people have been paying millions of dollars to make reservations on the first commercial space flight! Yet Vodka, on the other hand still comes in bottles from Russia, and will still turn a person into a zombie in about an hour. After an hour a day for a year, that zombie will say, "who me, I don't have a problem!" Denial to addictions, no matter what the addiction is, hasn't changed at all since the beginning of time. When an addict is caught stealing medications from a hospital or doctors office, they'll plead that the hospitals or doctors either shouldn't have them, or should keep them more secured! When a drunk driver hits and kills an innocent other driver, or even a pedestrian, the drunk driver will say that they had the right of way, that the victim was in their way, or had no right being there, or they had the green light, or didn't see the stop sign, etc., etc.! One excuse after another, but always insisting that it wasn't their fault.

    Denial is the clearest indication of the insanity of drug and alcohol use and abuse. There are many indicators of denial. The leading indicator of denial may just be the pure ignorance displayed in the often heard comments similar to "who me, what problem, I don't have a problem," etc., as the addict or alcoholic sits in an alley in a puddle of his own puke, or as he wakes up in a hospital after an overdose, or is being thrown out of his home because he can't pay his rent. He insists he doesn't have a problem as he gets rejected for the tenth time for a job interview because of his poor work history due to his addictions. Eventually he wakes up homeless, friendless, jobless, and penniless, sick, dying, and feeling hopeless. The epitome of drunkenness grown out of control.

    This is a form of pride, and pride in itself is sin, even though few see it that way. Pride blinds and paralyzes us into believing that we are in control of our own destiny. For man to believe that he's in control of his own destiny is in itself a form of insanity, convincing himself that he is his own god, and certainly has no need for the True Living God, who in fact, is his only way out of this delusion. Every day we see billionaires, celebrities, sports stars, rock stars, famous Politicians, even church leaders in the news because of succumbing to addictions, and losing everything they own, sometimes ending up as homeless alcoholics and addicts, or in jail or prison, we should easily recognize that we have no control over our own destiny. Yet pride keeps millions of alcoholics and addicts in denial even from this simple truth and reality.

Pride leads to denial, and then relapse. (Prov. 3:7, 16:18) Denial is pride! (Romans 12:3 , Prov. 11:2) Without God's Grace and humility, we'll never get beyond denial, and until we do, we'll never find Eternal recovery! There's nothing on this earth more impossible for a man to do, than to admit that there's something he *can't* do! That's pride, and arrogance! Hence: Addiction, "we can't just say no to a problem if we don't believe we have a problem!" Or, if and when we finally admit that we do have one, we believe that we can fix it ourselves without anyone else's help! Millions suffer with addictions to the brink of death because of pride. Our unwillingness to admit that we have a problem that we can't fix or control, is little less than suicide. We'll gamble our lives, health, careers, fortunes, and even our families, for the sake of pride and denial. Pride is sin, just as addiction is sin. Until we learn how to recognize it and how it operates and affects us, we'll never be able to begin to over-come it.

Pride doesn't just reside in the alcoholic and addict, but in all human beings, and it controls every man's life until they learn to control it. For alcoholics and addicts, it becomes the dominating factor in our denial. For most alcoholics and addicts, in the early stages of their addictions, a very common comment heard in meetings around the world millions of times every day is, "*I*" can quit drinking or using drugs anytime "*I*" choose to!"

There can *never* be any recovery until that person recognizes the lie and deceit in such a comment. They've not yet come to the realization of the power satan has over them through drugs and alcohol, and other sin. And it's pride that keeps them from seeing the Truth and reality of their circumstances. No one wants to face the guilt, shame, embarrassment, and stigma of the reality that your weakness has allowed the devil to consume you and your entire life. But you must face that reality before you can begin to conquer your pride. Whether you're a teenager not wanting to disappoint your parents, friends, or other peers, or a 50 year old successful business man not wanting to expose your true identity for many obvious reasons, or if you're someone in thousands of other similar circumstances, it's always pride, that keeps everyone in the same state of denial, that they don't have a problem that they can't fix themselves!

Complacency will also lead to denial and then relapse. While the continuous dark times of addictions will eventually lead some of us out of denial, and into recovery, the good times that can follow, if we're not extremely cautious, can often lead us into complacency, and right back into relapse. We need a solid, close personal relationship with Christ, and fellowship with other Christians, to keep us from that tragedy. We need to stay grounded in God's Word, The Truth, (Mat. 22:37, 2 Tim. 2:22 , James 1:12 , James 5:16 , 1 John 1:3, 1:7), to grow and maintain our Faith which will keep us humble and prevent complacency. We need "thorns", as Paul did in 2 Corinthians 12:7, to keep from becoming "conceited," or complacent. We need to recognize that sin is always just around the corner, and satan, the master of deceit, is always waiting for us to let our guard down and give in to temptation. 1 Peter 5:8, "Be sober, be vigilant; because your adversary the devil, as a roaring lion, walketh about, seeking whom he may devour"

Another form of denial used by many in addictions, is to build themselves a "closet" to hide in! The fact that most alcoholics and addicts learn early on how to become human chameleons, they can be very creative in creating false identities and environments to escape from the reality of their addictions. It astounds me at how many times I've discovered some very successful, talented, and gifted individuals who spend years hiding their addictions from everyone around them. Their spouses and children, their closest friends, their co-workers, their pastors, or even in some cases, the pastors parishioners, discover after years of association, that they've been deceived. All too often this discovery is made because of some significant life changing circumstance or tragedy that ends up destroying the various relationships. Many alcoholics and addicts will move from job to job, church to church, town to town, and even spouse to spouse, in order to keep their "secret" hidden. You can move 10,000 miles away to escape reality, but nothing will change if you bring your old baggage with you. A big part of stepping out of denial is learning to leave our baggage behind. It's self-destructive to carry it with us.

Denial takes on many masks of identity. Addicts become masters of deception like chameleons. You can be Bob one minute, and Bill the next! The epitome of Dr. Jekyll and Mr. Hyde. Until denial is recognized, acknowledged and overcome, addiction recovery can't begin. Denial is barricading ourselves and our emotions behind the walls that we build to hide and block out the pain and trauma of the reality we've experienced growing up. While we're hiding behind those walls, or in the "closet" we've created, we inhibit our ability to grow and mature emotionally, and as Christians, our ability to mature spiritually. In order to tear down those walls, and escape from the prison we've been hiding in, we must learn to surrender and trust God with every fiber of our being. He is our only Hope. The only source of everlasting sobriety.

Hopelessness is the result of the absence of Jesus Christ in our lives. Hopelessness becomes another form of denial. Hopelessness is the most destructive weapon satan has in his arsenal against alcoholics and addicts. There is nothing but despair in a life that's consumed with the hopelessness of addictions. Yet millions of the most wounded, and damaged lost souls, whose lives have been, and are being destroyed every minute of every day to addictions, are being held captive by 12-step addiction recovery programs that teach the lie that is heard around the world, "once a drunk, always a drunk"! A despicably hopeless statement that is promoted as the truth to millions of alcoholics and addicts in addiction recovery meetings around the world every day. And alcoholics and addicts wonder why they relapse, as the rest of the world wonders why there's such a big problem with addictions. For a Christian in a Church to hear those words, "once a drunk always a drunk," is like telling them that they're "forever condemned," or can't be "set free" from that sin.

Hopelessness ends up becoming part of the denial process when a person decides that since they have no hope, i.e., "once a drunk, always a drunk," they convince themselves, "why should I even bother trying, woe is me, I'll never beat this, I might as well give up," etc., etc. This kind of negative thinking will lead an addict into denying that they're in denial! "I'm not in denial, I'm just a hopeless drunk or addict." Denial grows like cancer, and is fed every time someone tells them that they have a problem, and is unprepared to spend the necessary time to explain to them, why or how they have a problem, and that there is Hope! You shouldn't tell an alcoholic or an addict that they have a problem unless you can show them that there is Hope! And what that Hope is, and where they can find it.

Our society has been sweeping this "hopeless" and "anonymous" segment of the population under the rug for decades. While the numbers of alcoholics and addicts are in the millions, they have no voice in the world because the system in which they exist, keeps them "anonymous." The AA 12-step program, which dominates the entire recovery world, is founded on the idea of anonymity, which is the reason why the general public has no idea how serious the problem of drug and alcohol use and abuse is in the world, unless they're unfortunate enough to have some personal experience with it. Anonymity promotes, at least subconsciously, the idea that one should keep their addictions a secret. We can't move beyond denial until we can face ourselves in the mirror, and admit to ourselves who we are, and that we have a serious problem. A problem that requires immediate attention. The longer we hide behind the mask of anonymity, the longer we stay in denial!

The AA theory of "once a drunk, always a drunk," and another lie that they promote, the theory that drunkenness is a disease, creates negative thinking which results in hopelessness, often leading to depression, isolation, and far too often, to the epitome of hopelessness, which is suicide. Many of those who have spent years living in this hopelessness and the consequences of their addictions, end up taking their own lives. Often through obvious means such as intentionally overdosing, which is easily detected, or using a gun, or jumping into the path of an oncoming vehicle. A much more subtle method is simply ignoring a doctor's report of failing health that could lead to death. Many keep drinking in spite of the knowledge that their liver or other organs are failing and if they don't quit drinking or doing drugs, they will die. These victims of addictions are also the victims of the same failed addiction recovery system that simply sweeps the records of these deaths under the rug so the general public has no idea of the seriousness of the problem. The coroner's report will list the cause of death as "natural." There are no hard numbers or statistics, on these deaths and others related to drug and alcohol use and abuse, because of a lack of interest and compassion for this lost and "anonymous" segment of our society.

Hopelessness, which is the direct result of the absence of Jesus Christ in 90% of our addiction recovery programs, is the reason we can't overcome and defeat addictions. AA lures many into its meetings, and entices churches into starting their own AA meetings based on another lie, that they have Christian roots, yet refuses to promote and share The Gospel Truth of God's Word, the Bible, in any of its meetings. Any church leader who claims to be a Born Again Christian, and then allows someone or some program to rob their flock of hope by convincing them that they're powerless, hopeless, and that their sin is a disease, hasn't read the words of Jesus in Acts 1:8, "But you will receive *power* when the Holy Spirit comes on you; and you will be my witnesses in Jerusalem, and in all Judea and Samaria, and to the ends of the earth." Or in Philippians 4:13, "I can do ***all*** things through Christ which ***strengtheneth me***." Or we read in 1 Pet. 1:3: "Give praise to the GOD and father of our Lord Jesus Christ. In *HIS* great mercy he has given us a new birth and a *"hope"* that is alive". We, who belong to Christ, have ***"hope"!*** The Bible is filled with scripture teaching us of the *"hope"* that we have,…here are just a few more,… Romans 15:4 NIV, "For everything that was written in the past was written to teach us, so that through the endurance taught in the Scriptures and the encouragement they provide we might have *"hope."* Romans 15:13 NIV, "May the God of *"hope"* fill you with all joy and peace as you trust in him, so that you may overflow with *"hope"* by the *"power"* of the Holy Spirit." So again I say, We who belong to Christ, have *"Hope"*!

With the "*Faith"* of a mustard seed, and the *"Hope"* of Christ Crucified, a repentant Heart, and obedience to God's Word and will for us, His Word promises us that we will be ***SAVED and SOBER!***

CHAPTER 9

Enabling

Another powerful weapon in the devils arsenal

Proverbs 19:18
"Discipline your son, for in that there is hope; do not be a willing party to his death."

Enabling an alcoholic or an addict is typically, or most often, done within the home by a family member. A loved one whose motives are out of love, and intensions are meant to benefit their loved ones, not hurt them. It usually starts at an early age and stage of one's addictions, when a mom or dad or both don't recognize the symptoms of their child's bad behavior as being anything more than that, "bad behavior," or "typical teenage behavior." It usually begins as little more than spoiling the child and letting them do whatever they want. It doesn't take the child very long to know who's in charge! This sets up a disastrous scenario if and when the child is tempted by peers to try and experiment with drugs and alcohol. Once they're addicted, they'll become masters of deception. As cunning as a fox, and whose actions are hidden like a chameleon! The parents are often the last ones to know that their own children have become alcoholics or addicts. And 9 times out of 10, they've been enabling them by providing them with the money or other resources that they need. The other resources being transportation, and freedom. Or complete lack of oversight in whom their children hang out with. There's another whole chapter still to come on the complexities of parenting in the world of drugs and alcohol.

Another common "breeding ground" if you will, for enabling, outside of the home, and yet close to everyone concerned, might be when a hard-working, devoted husband, and loving father, and church member, stumbles into the pastor's office one day admitting an addiction! It doesn't matter if it's a tiny little country church in a town of 50, or a giant, big city mega-church of thousands of members and a huge staff, *few* are equipped to handle this kind of tragedy adequately! Few will be familiar enough with addictions to know how to deal with enabling. In fact, not being equipped to adequately counsel an alcoholic or an addict scripturally using God's Word and Truth will in itself be a form of enabling. It will send a message to the addict that God can't help, and build on his feeling of hopelessness.

Not only is addiction a tragedy, but it's also become in recent years an epidemic! Why are most churches ill-equipped to handle such vital, potentially deadly circumstances? For one thing, the church itself in many cases has been in denial of the problem until recently when it grew into such an epidemic, they could no longer ignore it. Then, 90% of the folks in your church who may have a problem with an addiction, are in denial, and don't admit it. Most pastors or counselors hear about a member's addictions from a spouse first. Then you have two problems! The addicted spouse feels betrayed and is as angry as a hornet! So you have a much bigger problem than you can begin to imagine. Addictions can be a silent and invisible killer sometimes, well masked and disguised by the addict until it's so far out of control, when it is revealed, it's a shock to everyone involved. Many times hidden addictions are revealed through tragedies such as someone ending up in jail or a serious accident, or develop a health problem related to alcohol. Then, the spouse, or co-worker, or friend claims to have had no idea that so-and-so had a problem, or if they did know, they were in denial themselves, and were consequently enabling the other person. These are just a few of the many obstacles facing a Pastor or church counselor.

First, it's not until the addiction is revealed that we can begin to move forward and face the challenge of "denial". An alcoholic or addict might spend years in denial. Their world might be crashing down all around them, obvious to everyone else around them, but they'll refuse to acknowledge that they have a problem. It seems to almost always take a tragedy of some sort to hit a low enough "bottom", to get an addicts attention. Trying to help someone who's still in denial is like trying to convince a child they shouldn't play with a loaded gun! And ignoring an addict can have the same devastating results as allowing a child to play with a loaded gun! Sooner or later, they'll kill themselves or someone else! Second, you have the codependents who are usually in denial themselves, hence, their "enabling". Third, overcoming denial is just the first step of many in a very long journey that will require endless amounts of patience and love from us, and Gods infinite Love, Wisdom, and Grace, which He promises will overcome our trials through Faith. And fourth, the church itself actually becomes a codependent by definition, since the addict becomes dependent upon the church for help and assistance. A very big responsibility indeed! Even the church itself, must turn its ear inwards and listen to its own message. Only God has the Power, Love, and Grace to "Set Free" an alcoholic or an addict. And only a Christ centered, Gospel based church can deliver His Message to the ones who need to hear it. Most churches today, can barely keep up with the growing crisis of broken marriages and the related issues that brings on our youth, the children of the broken families. Ironically, a great number of these issues, (broken marriages), can usually be traced back to some form of addictions as a root cause.

    The reason I've written this book, is a concern that I have had for quite some time over the way in which the church, in general, has addressed the issue of addiction recovery. I believe the church, under so much pressure to do *"something"* to address this crisis, turned to what they thought was the only tool available to them at the time, and without adequate research, allowed a secular 12-step addiction recovery program into their churches. 12-step recovery started with one program, (A/A), and has now grown into the Heinz 47 varieties. They, A/A, began with a purely secular foundation, straight out of the world, but claiming to be Christian based, however filled with lies and heresy! How, for one second, can you expect to spiritually counsel the Born Again church member sitting in front of your desk, by telling them that he or she has a disease, or that they're powerless, and have no hope? These are 3 basic fundamental principles that are part of the A/A program, and most other 12-step programs. Using this program in a Christian Church would be the ultimate case of "enabling"! And a big part of the problem for the epidemic and rise of addictions, rather than a decrease. If the huge increase in recent years in recovery programs, treatment facilities, and group homes were working, we should be seeing a significant decrease in the problem, rather than the exponential, out-of-control, epidemic we're experiencing today. It's perfectly clear that the secular, worldly, philosophical methods of recovery are a failure. The Church should be the answer, yet it's also failing because it's chosen to incorporate worldly philosophy. Colossians 2:8 (KJV), "Beware lest any man spoil you through philosophy and vain deceit, after the tradition of men, after the rudiments of the world, and not after Christ."

The fact is, that A/A has in the past, since its inception, and still today officially, ***"proclaims"*** to be a Christian institution, yet, however denies Christ, and refuses to allow the Gospel to be shared at its meetings for fear of insulting or hurting a non believers feelings. (Jude 1:4), "For certain men whose condemnation was written about long ago have secretly slipped in among you. They are godless men, who change the grace of our God into a license for immorality and deny Jesus Christ our only Sovereign and Lord". Also see 2 John 1:7, "Many deceivers, who do not acknowledge Jesus Christ as coming in the flesh, have gone out into the world. Any such person is the deceiver and the antichrist." Sadly, AA has been very successful in worming its way into many churches today, deceiving many pastors and counselors, whose walls are cluttered with useless degrees, and documents of achievement, yet have little if any real world experience, which is what's needed in dealing with the hurting, broken lives of alcoholics and addicts. Sirs, if you believe that sharing secular addiction recovery programs, and their philosophy is an acceptable standard for Christian counseling, they're looking for help at Wal-Mart!

Seriously, the number of victims, (often the enablers), affected or impacted by the alcoholic or addict, either directly or indirectly, is widespread, and quite often they end up just as wounded and scarred as the addict. Just like it is in any war, alcohol and drug addiction *is* Spiritual warfare, and there end up being many casualties. The wounds go far beyond, and are much deeper than what the layman, or inexperienced counselor or mentor can recognize. Many times, a victim, (codependent), may suffer deeper wounds than the alcoholics or addicts themselves. Over a period of time, the alcoholic or addict will become insensitive to their emotions and feelings. The nature of addiction itself seems to greatly affect and erode the emotions and senses of most addicts. Whereas the spouse, parent, child, siblings, or other friends and colleagues of the addict, initially, at least, are able to maintain to some degree, some sort of emotional stability. Eventually, however, even the strongest codependent will begin to bend under the stress brought on by the addictions of their friends or loved ones without some solid help from another source. *Enabling* will always draw the *enabler* into the pit of despair over time.

    As Christians involved in addiction recovery, no matter what our relationship is with an addict or an alcoholic, God is very clear about the fact that we must rebuke and correct our brothers and sisters in Christ who have fallen into sin. 2 Timothy 4:2 says, ***Preach the word; be instant in season, out of season; reprove, rebuke, exhort with all long suffering and doctrine.*** Every Christian has the responsibility to rebuke, warn, and correct another Christian of their wayward behavior. According to Ezekiel 3:17-19, *¹⁷ "Son of man, I have made you a watchman for the people of Israel; so hear the word I speak and give them warning from me. ¹⁸ When I say to a wicked person, 'You will surely die,' and you do not warn them or speak out to dissuade them from their evil ways in order to save their life, that wicked person will die for their sin, and I will hold you accountable for their blood. ¹⁹ But if you do warn the wicked person and they do not turn from their wickedness or from their evil ways, they will die for their sin; but you will have saved yourself.*

Ezekiel 33:9 says, *But if you do warn the wicked person to turn from their ways and they do not do so, they will die for their sin, though you yourself will be saved.* On the other hand, Titus 3:10 is clear that we shouldn't extend a "long leash," that after two warnings we should move on. Titus 3:10, *"Warn a divisive person once, and then warn them a second time. After that, have nothing to do with them."* I suspect the message here is that there needs to be a line drawn in the sand before we cross into enabling our brothers and sisters. At some point we need to learn to "shake the dust off our sandals," (Math.10:14, Acts 13:51), and let God deal with the individual. We can be assured that there will be many who will not want to hear the Truth. And the Truth is very clear, Heb.3:13, 1 Cor.4:14, Gal.5:20-22, 2 Tim.4:2, Titus 1:13, 2:15, Prov.15:32, Eph.5:11, 1 Tim.5:19-21, 1 Cor.5:11-13, is just some of the scripture that instructs us to rebuke and correct our brothers and sisters who are struggling with addictions. When we don't follow God's instructions, we are enabling them.

We can be assured that whenever we attempt to correct or warn someone who is caught in sinful addictions and behavior, they most likely will respond out of denial and accuse us of "judging them!" Rather than backing down in defeat for fear of rejection, we must respond with a resounding "yes, I'm judging you," as directed by God's Word in, 1 Corinthians 5:12-13, 12 *"What business is it of mine to judge those outside the church? Are you not to judge those inside? 13 God will judge those outside. "Expel the wicked person from among you."* Or, 1 Cor. 6:2-3, 2 *"Or do you not know that the Lord's people will judge the world? And if you are to judge the world, are you not competent to judge trivial cases? 3 Do you not know that we will judge angels? How much more the things of this life!"* Paul also instructs us in 1Timothy 5:19-21, 19

"Do not entertain an accusation against an elder unless it is brought by two or three witnesses. 20 But those elders who are sinning you are to reprove before everyone, so that the others may take warning. 21 I charge you, in the sight of God and Christ Jesus and the elect angels, to keep these instructions without partiality, and to do nothing out of favoritism." And again in, 2 Timothy 4:1-3, *"In the presence of God and of Christ Jesus, who will judge the living and the dead, and in view of his appearing and his kingdom, I give you this charge: 2 Preach the word; be prepared in season and out of season; correct, rebuke and encourage—with great patience and careful instruction. 3 For the time will come when people will not put up with sound doctrine. Instead, to suit their own desires, they will gather around them a great number of teachers to say what their itching ears want to hear."* Again, it is our responsibility to admonish and correct our brothers and sisters when we witness them being overcome by the temptations of the enemy, according to Ezekiel 3: 17-19, and 33:9.

Most Christians will do everything within their power to avoid confrontation with other Christians. Yet rebuking and correcting another will almost always lead to confrontation because of pride. We're living in times when false teaching is rampant in our churches today, and millions of Christians in various addiction recovery programs have been mislead for years into believing that they're powerless, in spite of Jesus' own words in Acts 1:8, *"But ye shall receive **power**, after that the Holy Ghost is come upon you: and ye shall be witnesses unto me both in Jerusalem, and in all Judaea, and in Samaria, and unto the uttermost part of the earth."* How can we call ourselves Christians, if we're not going to believe Jesus' own words? That's why we must be prepared to admonish one another with scripture, out of Love, through prayer, and God's Grace. Colossians 3:16, *"Let the word of Christ dwell in you richly in all wisdom; teaching and admonishing one another in psalms and hymns and spiritual songs, singing with grace in your hearts to the Lord."* This can be a daunting challenge when mentoring alcoholics and addicts who are in denial. Many will refuse to listen. That's why we have scripture like Titus 3:10 to help guide us, Titus 3:10 (NIV) *"Warn a divisive person once, and then warn them a second time. After that, have nothing to do with them."* If we don't follow these instructions, we risk crossing the line into becoming enablers ourselves.

The hardest thing for the Christian enabler is that sometimes the only way to cope with alcoholics and addicts is not through our natural Christ like instinct of Love and patience, but through tough Love and confrontation. Can we Love our neighbor or loved one, and still not answer their phone call, or return or respond to the message, "Mom, I'm in jail again, or I need some money for this, that, or the other? We must set clear boundaries, and not waver from them every time our friend or loved one rejects our attempts to reach out. We must learn to let them suffer the consequences of their behavior, rather than bailing them out of one trial after another. As Christians, we must recognize that God expects all of us to endure the consequences of the trials He sends our way according to His will, when we are disobedient. And He wants us to learn to become completely reliant on Him for strength, rather than relying on a friend or loved one. If we bail a loved one out of jail, or help them find a new job, or pay their rent or car payment, or loan them some money, over and over again because of their actions that are a result of their addictions, we're not only enabling the them, but may very well be hindering and interfering with Gods work in that person's life. Letting our addicted friends or loved ones manipulate us into enabling them will only prolong their recovery, and add to their pain and suffering from the consequences that will follow.

    The Good News is that there's only one reliable, absolute source of guaranteed recovery for both the addict and the enabler, who becomes the silent victim, or codependent. That source is our total surrender into the Loving arms of our Lord and Savior Jesus Christ! I try to address as many of these issues of enabling as I'm aware of, and do it in a way, and in terms that a layman might relate to and understand. This is not easy work. To minister to someone who's entire life may have been under the influence of alcohol, or some other deadly, mind-altering narcotic, or other life destroying sin, can only be done successfully with and through the Love and Grace and Power of Jesus Christ! Period! And with the patience that only He can provide us. There is no other Power on earth that can kick the Devil out of a wounded addict! Once we've discovered, and accepted this simple Truth, repented, surrendered, and turned to God for deliverance, can we be **SAVED and SOBER!**

CHAPTER 10

Mentoring

Next to his personal relationship with God, an addict's best weapon against addictions is a good mentor and fellowship.

2 Timothy 1:1-2;
*"You then, my son, be strong in the grace that is in Christ Jesus. And the things you have heard me say in the presence of many witnesses entrust to reliable men who will also be qualified to **teach** others."*
Ephesians 4:7;
But to each one of us grace has been given as Christ apportioned it.
Ephesians 4:11-13;
*So Christ himself gave the apostles, the prophets, the evangelists, the pastors and **teachers**, 12 to equip his people for works of service, so that the body of Christ may be built up 13 until we all reach unity in the faith and in the knowledge of the Son of God and become **mature**, attaining to the whole measure of the fullness of Christ.*
Philippians 1:7
*It is right for me to feel this way about all of you, since I have you in my heart and, whether I am in chains or defending and confirming the gospel, all of you **share** in God's grace with me.*
Colossians 1:12

*and giving joyful thanks to the Father, who has qualified you to **share** in the inheritance of his holy people in the kingdom of light.*
1 Thessalonians 2:8
*so we cared for you. Because we loved you so much, we were delighted to **share** with you not only the gospel of God but our lives as well.*
2 Thessalonians 2:14
*He called you to this through our gospel, that you might **share** in the glory of our Lord Jesus Christ.*
1 Timothy 6:18
*Command them to do good, to be rich in good deeds, and to be generous and willing to **share**.*
Philemon 1:6
*I pray that your partnership with us in the faith may be effective in deepening your understanding of every good thing we **share** for the sake of Christ.*
Hebrews 3:14
*We have come to **share** in Christ, if indeed we hold our original conviction firmly to the very end.*
Hebrews 13:16
*And do not forget to do good and to **share** with others, for with such sacrifices God is pleased.*

Definition: Mentor: A wise, experienced, and trusted counselor, advisor, or teacher. At some point after we've become Saved and Sober, God will call us to mentor others. The word mentor is used to describe individuals usually found in Christian addiction recovery programs, who have been chosen to disciple other men and women who are just beginning their long journey of addiction recovery. A mentors primary mission is to share not only the Good News of The Gospel, but their own personal "good news," or story of deliverance, or testimony of how God freed them from their bondage to addictions, allowing them to be Saved and Sober. (1 Thessalonians 2:8, "so we cared for you. Because we loved you so much, we were delighted to **share** with you not only the gospel of God but our lives as well.")

Looking back at my many years of Christian addiction recovery counseling, which followed many earlier years in many meeting rooms of AA meetings, where that position was known as being a "sponsor." Today, thinking back to the word "sponsor," and what it meant in secular 12-step recovery programs brings much hesitation, apprehension, and amazement. Rarely did I ever find anyone who met the criteria to be considered a counselor or advisor or teacher. In an "A" typical 12-step AA meeting, it seems that the only qualification to be a "sponsor" was for someone to have a day's more sobriety than the person seeking a sponsor. This policy seemed to me to be much too much like the "blind leading the blind"! A train wreck waiting for a place to happen! A sure recipe for disaster! It also seemed to me, that most of the men and women who *thought* they were qualified to be a sponsor, were extremely self-righteous, even pious, sanctimonious, pompous, hypocrites, in need them-selves of a true humble mentor. There were a number of occasions when a sponsor would relapse just a short time into his/her role sponsoring someone else! It was not unusual to encounter men who thought being a sponsor was an opportunity to seduce female members in their groups! Unfortunately over a period of time, entrapped, and mired in the quicksand of secular 12-step programs, you get accustomed to, and even expecting such behavior. This is just another of the many reasons to keep secular, 12-step recovery programs out of our churches!

The mentoring programs in a Christian Church's addiction recovery program needs to be prayed over, and scrutinized by the leaders of the Church.

A sponsor from a secular 12-step addiction recovery program that's being used in the Christian community all too often could be a wolf in sheep's clothing! It would be a fair assessment and assumption that *most* Christians in these addiction recovery programs, who've been in bondage to their addictions for a lengthy period of time, would be considered somewhat immature in their Christian journey. It could prove perilous to partner them with a wolf in sheep's clothing, or even with another newly recovered or immature Christian. Given the deadly nature of addictions to drug and alcohol use and abuse, and the damaging nature of addictions to lead to other sinful behavior, mentoring must be taken very seriously by all concerned parties. Successful recovery, although promised by God in John 8:31-36 is a conditional promise and anyone seeking to be "set free" from the bondage of sin will require a thorough understanding of God's Word. Discipleship with humility, Love, patience, and understanding is an absolute prerequisite for the mentoring of any Christian struggling with addictions.

To be Saved and Sober we must recognize the importance and serious nature of the role of "mentors." Ultimately, other people's lives and welfare are at stake, as well as their Spiritual growth and maturity. A Christian addiction recovery program must have a structured, Christ centered, discipleship program based on the Gospel Truth of Christ and His scriptural precepts and doctrine. Not on secular 12-step "Big Book" philosophy. The primary prerequisite for mentors needs to be first and foremost, humility, followed by a mature and faithful relationship with their Lord and Savior, as well as their amount of time sober and or in recovery. Serious and prayerful consideration by leaders, (elders) needs to go into the assigning of mentors based on individuals needs. Everyone is at a different level of maturity and sanctification in their walk with the Lord, as well as their progress in recovery, and that needs to be taken into consideration when assigning a mentor. Next to God's Word, and revealed Truth, the mentoring program may be the most important element of a person's recovery process.

Another significant prerequisite to be qualified for mentoring is that we've had enough time in sobriety to have shed our emotional baggage. A difficult and time consuming task that is in direct proportion to how long we've been struggling with our addictions. The longer we're active in our addictions, the more baggage we acquire. Over the years we've accumulated many relational failures, secret sins, low self-esteem and emotional wounds from family, friends, co-workers and loved ones. This baggage has been hindering our own recovery for years, and we certainly can't expect to mentor others while still being burdened with our own dark shadows and memories. The closer we get to God, in our relationship with Him, the easier it is to let go of the past. Then He will position us to disciple others. And we must be absolutely sure that it is He who is doing the positioning and not us.

A big part of mentoring, is listening. (James 1:19) We must learn to listen with our hearts as well as our ears. We must be able to understand first, that the person we're listening to is reaching out to God through us. We must see ourselves as nothing more than a sponge that God has placed in this person's life to absorb their pain and heartache that their unloading on God. That He might understand them, not realizing He already does. But it's crucial that we just listen, especially in the early stages of recovery. It's important that we get to know and understand who we're mentoring, and as best as possible recognize how and why they're where they are. It would be foolish of us to offer any feedback other than encouragement until we know who's on the other side of the table.

Mentoring or discipling alcoholics and addicts will require us to be empowered with Gods fruit, (Gal. 5:22), to possess the utmost in humility, wisdom, patience, and an infinite understanding of the mind of an alcoholic or addict. Alcoholics and addicts, whether Christians or not, have acquired certain behavioral instincts that are distinct among them. Alcoholics and addicts quickly learn to become skilled at deception to the point of resembling a chameleon. They're experts at identity theft, putting on many masks throughout the day. Living lies, and lying become a way of life just to get through a day without revealing the truth as to their true identity, an addict, or an alcoholic. In spite of being psychologically wasted and high on drugs or drunk on alcohol, the guilt and stigma feed the denial that keeps them hiding from the truth and the reality of the dilemma they find themselves trapped in. The mentor must be able to see through the many masks of deception and lies, and discover the true identity of the person they're mentoring. No easy task for anyone without Gods Grace, wisdom, and guidance throughout what can be a very long and daunting task.

Because of denial, the mentor must patiently dissect the backgrounds of those they're mentoring all the way to the roots of early childhood, even infancy, before they start offering any specific advice, other than spiritual and scriptural Truth which always applies to everyone's state of well being. Many alcoholics and addicts problems began while they were still infants or very young children. Many grew up in homes where drug and alcohol use and abuse was present, possibly along with violence and abuse. One form of abuse that's prevalent in almost all children growing up in a home where drug and alcohol use and abuse was present, is the abuse of abandonment. While almost every parent, because of denial, will scream "foul," or "not me," the hard and sad truth is that when an alcoholic or addicted parent is high or drunk, they're not consciously present to be an adequate and responsible parent. They're AWOL, absent from their responsibility to raise their children, and Love and guide them. The more time they spend high or drunk, the greater the degree of abandonment. In many of these homes the younger children end up being raised by older siblings. So whether you're mentoring someone who is currently a parent in the midst of such a dilemma, or someone who grew up under such circumstances, your Love, patience, understanding and comfort will be crucial in building a relationship with this person whose consequence's have made it nearly impossible for them to trust anyone.

Trust, is crucial in the mentoring process. It's next to impossible to acquire someone's trust, yet vital to building a relationship with someone whose addictions have led them to distrust everyone. Almost everyone we mentor will have experienced the loss of everything important to them, family, friends, jobs, homes, everything material, often health, self-respect and esteem or dignity, and for many this has happened more than once. While still in denial, the alcoholic or addict will always blame someone else, never taking responsibility for it, instead, building a wall of distrust that will require a miracle to tear down, and making the job of a mentor that much more difficult, and the road to recovery that much more bumpy and painful. Trusting others, especially God is vital to recovery, yet blaming God is quite common.

Typically, most people who end up in addiction recovery, get started at an early age, and the basic reasons are because of a multitude of childhood circumstances, ranging from being raised in an abusive home, to simply hanging out with the wrong crowd. Today however, there's a brand new profile of addicts and alcoholics beginning to show up in various recovery meetings. In many cases it's an older crowd of folks who've become victims of our new "throw-away" society. Our new corporate culture of "disposable" executives and leaders, whose demise will benefit the employers coffers. Another large and growing group being found in addiction recovery meetings, are the many financially successful celebrities, sports stars, business leaders, and politicians, who are discovering that their millions or billions of dollars aren't enough to buy happiness. During the past few years we've witnessed millions of successful middle class Americans that have lost good paying jobs, savings, and their homes as a result. Many of these folks out of desperation, depression, and pain, have turned to drugs and alcohol to numb the pain, and many are now beginning to show up in addiction recovery meetings.

There are millions of Christians in addiction recovery programs, and *If* they can swallow enough pride to show up at a meeting in your Church, *"Trust"* will be a four letter word in their vocabulary that they won't want to hear! They'll feel betrayed by society in general, and some may be disappointed and feel betrayed by God. The most challenging task a mentor will face today is explaining to someone in recovery the reason they don't trust God and are blaming God for their troubles. Most people in recovery who are facing this dilemma are confronted with the same obstacles all Christians today are facing. A broken Church. A world overcome with churches that have drifted away from God, from His Truth, from The Gospel Message of Christ's shed blood on The Cross, and from the message of the need for repentance and obedience for Salvation. Churches that teach tolerance, and defense of our sinful nature, rather than repentance, churches that never mention or teach on "dirty" words or subjects such as repentance, sacrifice, trials, suffering, curses, sin, satan, hell, condemnation. Instead, most churches today are teaching lies and fairy tales of the hippie generation about love, peace, joy, and prosperity, and whatever else tickles your fancy. Lies about "fill our bank account and God will fill yours." The "name it and claim it" churches that have sprung up all over the country in the past few decades. Or "if you're not healed yet, you're not tithing enough. Many are still teaching the old doctrines of indulgences that you can buy your Salvation. If your "mentee" has been subjected to these conditions of false teachings, you have your work cut out for you. Your success will truly require that both of you draw near to the Lord in Prayer, meditation, and Faithful devotion, seeking His guidance and Grace.

    Another great challenge a mentor will face, are the many Christians in addiction recovery who actually have been betrayed and abandoned by their church for whatever reason. Not just those who "think" their difficulties were caused by God, but those who have been genuinely betrayed by a Church. The world today is filled with millions of people who have been abandoned or betrayed in some way by their Church. They've lost all respect and trust for their church and some will blame God and turn away from Him, rather than recognizing that it was a false teacher that God might have sent to teach the individual a valuable lesson. Many, because of the pain and disillusionment caused by this abandonment, will turn to drugs and alcohol, and other sin, as they drift further and further away from God.

    In spite of the seriousness of this dilemma, (the condition of the church), many pastors and church leaders will allow anyone to lead recovery groups without recognizing or understanding the enormous responsibility involved in such a task. They need to diligently and prayerfully oversee any addiction recovery program they might include in their counseling efforts, and choose someone who is qualified and equipped with the right gifts of the Spirit, and has the personal experience to lead someone in this condition back into a relationship with Jesus, and the Church, to regain their Trust.

Often, counselors with degrees and certificates earned through studying mans philosophy, as well as Christian theology, are not in itself adequate qualifications for mentoring people with broken spirits, because some church leader has already betrayed them. Winning them back will take a lot more than a book educated counselor. The only "Book" these people need is the Bible. Winning them back, and mentoring's #1 qualification should be someone who's "been there, done that," and survived, and knows absolutely, 101% that it was *only* by the Grace of God that they've been set free from their addictions! Any qualifications beyond that should only be considered a bonus. Many of today's churches operate like corporate enterprises where degrees take precedence over experience and common sense. Far too many of our Church counselors today are equipped with little more than degrees and certificates earned through secular educational institutions, mixed with some theology, but with very little personal experience or on the job training.

For the smaller Church where the Pastor may also be the counselor and mentor, and has not personally experienced the wrath and devastation of addictions, he should do some homework and research before taking on such a formidable task. I hope this book might be insightful to the many individuals who find themselves in such a position.

Usually by the time an alcoholic or an addict reaches the point in recovery of reaching out to someone else for help, (once they've overcome denial), they're in a very sensitive and delicate state of mind and emotions. They need to be treated with "kids gloves," first, with Love and respect, patience and humility. *Never* tell someone at this stage of recovery that you know or understand where they are, or what they've been through, or are going through! Know and understand this,…you don't know, and they know you don't. No matter what your own personal experience was, it was yours, and only yours. Everyone's story is different, and your "mentee's" may teach you a valuable lesson.

A.W. Tozer wrote in a devotional once, "Distinguishing between Jacob and Esau", "There are areas of Christian thought, and because of thought then also of life, where likenesses and differences are so difficult to distinguish that we are often hard put to it to escape complete deception. Throughout the whole world error and truth travel the same highways, work in the same fields and factories, attend the same churches, fly in the same planes and shop in the same stores. So skilled is error at imitating truth that the two are constantly being mistaken for each other. It takes a sharp eye these days to know which brother is Cain and which Abel. We must never take for granted anything that touches our soul's welfare. Isaac felt Jacob's arms and thought they were the arms of Esau. Even the disciples failed to spot the traitor among them; the only one of them who knew who he was Judas himself. That soft-spoken companion with whom we walk so comfortably and in whose company we take such delight may be an angel of Satan, whereas that rough, plain-spoken man whom we shun may be God's very prophet sent to warn us against danger and eternal loss."   A.W. Tozer

A mentor must always be 100% honest and

realistic, never misleading or offering false hope or making any unrealistic promises. Every addict is different with different needs and strengths and weaknesses. Consequently, every mentor must be flexible and able to adjust their own strengths to meet the needs of the addict. The only way to do this is to be a prayer warrior, and complete reliance on The Holy Spirit for guidance.

This might be a larger responsibility than the pastors of smaller churches are capable of dealing with. In a typical Sunday morning service, the audience the pastor is facing is a group of people with clear minds, who have gathered to hear Gods Word and give Him Praise and worship. On the other hand, recovery group leaders are dealing with people who are just coming out of a fog and are trying to recover from the trauma of perhaps years of bondage to the sins of many addictions. Whether you're a pastor, a group leader, or a mentor, or all three, the task ahead will be daunting and challenging, and the responsibility at times, overwhelming. Without the presence of God in every meeting. Just as in our own personal lives, we can do nothing without Him, yet "all things" with Him!

While I stated above that "Mentoring's #1 qualification should be someone who's "been there, done that," and survived, and knows absolutely, 101% that it was ***only*** by the Grace of God that they've been set free from their addictions, and any qualifications beyond that should only be considered a bonus." That really should be the #2 qualification, because the first and foremost qualification must always be the mentors relationship with his Lord and Savior! A close personal relationship with Jesus, where there's been a complete 100% surrender to self and the world, were the mentor has taken up, and is carrying the Cross of Christ in His footsteps, and is anxious to wash the feet of the lost souls God has placed in his care, with this commitment, all other qualifications will be second nature. One who is following the guidance of The Holy Spirit, needs no other guidance. The gifts and needs for successful service will be provided by God according to His Will. Any assistance from man will only hinder the results.

We need to recognize the importance and serious nature of the role of "mentors." Ultimately, other people's lives, welfare, and future are at stake, as well as their Spiritual growth and maturity. The primary prerequisite for mentors needs to be a mature and faithful relationship with their Lord and Savior, as well as their amount of time sober and or in recovery. Serious and prayerful consideration by leaders, (elders) needs to go into the assigning of mentors based on individuals needs. Everyone is at a different level of maturity and sanctification in their walk with the Lord, as well as their progress in recovery, and that needs to be taken into consideration when assigning a mentor. Next to God's Word, and revealed Truth, a mentoring program may be the most important element of recovery, and in leading our members into Eternal Recovery with their Savior, Jesus Christ.
MENTORING 101; Luke 6:40, A student is not above his teacher, but everyone who is fully trained will be like his teacher.

A mentor will often times be filling the shoes of an absent parent, or one who was never present. For anyone in those circumstances, Ephesians 6:4 says, "Fathers, do not exasperate your children; instead, bring them up in the training and instruction of the Lord." Or, we could say, Mentors, "do not exasperate" those placed in your care.

Many alcoholics and addicts, in spite of their desperation to be set free from their addictions will reject any instruction from their mentors. For those mentors, Paul offers this advice, in 1 Thessalonians

4:8, "Therefore, he who rejects this instruction does not reject man but God, who gives you his Holy Spirit." At some point, you will encounter some-one who's just not ready to surrender and accept Gods Love, Blessings, and instruction. Your most difficult task in mentoring will be when it becomes necessary to accept Gods Words in 2 Thessalonians 3:13-15, 13, "And as for you, brothers, never tire of doing what is right. 14, If anyone does not obey our instruction in this letter, take special note of him. Do not associate with him, in order that he may feel ashamed. 15, Yet do not regard him as an enemy, but warn him as a brother." There will be times when it will be necessary to cut ties and go in different directions. A wise Mentor will know when these times arise, and accomplish it with dignity and Love. The ideal situation whenever possible would be to simply change mentors, but this may not always be an option. We must Trust God to lead us to make the right choice. Many alcoholics and addicts are just not ready for change, or to surrender completely to God. Some want to hang onto their earthly treasures and pleasures a little longer, no matter how much damage they're doing to themselves.

    Another situation that we as mentors must always be aware of, is that sometimes Gods not finished with the process of the "refiners fire" in someone's life. There will be many occasions when we need to learn when to "stand down," or step aside, and let God do what He knows is best for those in recovery. We need to be able to recognize when we might be interfering with His work or plans in the individuals life. Sanctification is Gods job, not ours. Basically, our job is simply to be a messenger for god, to deliver His instructions either through His Word, or *our* actions.

    Sometimes the message He's trying to share with others might be for *our* benefit as well as theirs. We can learn much from watching God work in others lives, recognizing that He's in control, and that we need to step aside and mind our own business. In recovery, as with anything in life, it's often about "letting go, and letting God" take control of our lives. That often means waiting on God. (Psalm 27:14, "Wait patiently for the Lord. Be brave and courageous. Yes, wait patiently for the Lord.") The "refiners fire," (Malachi 3:3, "And he shall sit as a refiner and purifier of silver: and he shall purify the sons of Levi, and purge them as gold and silver, that they may offer unto the Lord an offering in righteousness."), plays a very important role, not only in our recovery, but in the quality of our recovery, and in our lives and relationship with God. If it were not for our trials, and the way we respond to them, we would all be responding to His words, "Ye of little Faith"! As mentors, we must always be showing diligence and vigilance in our efforts to assist God in _His_ work with those He places in our path, recognizing at all times that we're merely tools and instruments in His hands that He's using to fulfill His will in their lives. Through humility, we must never lose sight of who we are in Him, merely servants, and as mentors in addiction recovery, we should consider these words of Christ in Luke 4:18, *"The Spirit of the Lord is upon me, for He has anointed me to bring Good News to the poor. He has sent me to proclaim that captives will be released, that the blind will see, that the oppressed will be set free."*

    A mentor must examine, study, meditate and pray over as much scripture as God will lead him to before beginning his service as a mentor, here's a small sampling of some scripture that will be helpful to begin with,...
Acts 2:41-43 NIV, Those who accepted his message were baptized, and about three thousand were added to their number that day. 42, They devoted

themselves to the apostles' *teaching* and to the *fellowship*, to the breaking of bread and to prayer. 43, Everyone was filled with awe, and many wonders and miraculous signs were done by the apostles.

Romans 12:6-8 NIV, We have different gifts, according to the grace given us. If a man's gift is prophesying, let him use it in proportion to his faith. 7 If it is serving, let him serve; if it is *teaching*, let him *teach*; 8 if it is *encouraging*, let him *encourage*; if it is contributing to the needs of others, let him give generously; if it is leadership, let him govern diligently; if it is showing mercy, let him do it cheerfully.

Ephesians 4:11-13, So Christ himself gave the apostles, the prophets, the evangelists, the pastors and *teachers*, 12 to equip his people for works of service, so that the body of Christ may be built up 13 until we all reach unity in the faith and in the knowledge of the Son of God and become *mature*, attaining to the whole measure of the fullness of Christ.

Colossians 3:16, Let the word of Christ dwell in you richly as you *teach* and admonish one another with all wisdom, and as you sing psalms, hymns and spiritual songs with gratitude in your hearts to God.

1 Timothy 3:1-3 NIV, Overseers and Deacons, Here is a trustworthy saying: If anyone sets his heart on being an overseer, he desires a noble task. 2 Now the overseer must be above reproach, the husband of but one wife, temperate, self-controlled, respectable, hospitable, able to *teach*, 3 not given to *drunkenness*, not violent but gentle, not quarrelsome, not a lover of money.

Titus 2:1-2 What Must Be Taught to Various Groups, You must *teach* what is in accord with sound doctrine. 2, *Teach* the older men to be temperate, worthy of respect, self-controlled, and sound in faith, in love and in endurance.

Titus 2:7-8 In everything set them an example by doing what is good. In your *teaching* show integrity, seriousness, 8, and soundness of speech that cannot be condemned, so that those who oppose you may be ashamed because they have nothing bad to say about us. Titus 2:15, These, then, are the things you should *teach*. ***Encourage and rebuke*** with all authority. Do not let anyone despise you.

1 John 2:27, As for you, the anointing you received from him remains in you, and you do not need anyone to *teach* you. But as his anointing *teaches* you about all things and as that anointing is real, not counterfeit—just as it has *taught* you, remain in him.

Ephesians 6:4, Fathers, do not exasperate your children; instead, bring them up in the training and instruction of the Lord.

1 Thessalonians 4:8, Therefore, he who rejects this instruction does not reject man but God, who gives you his Holy Spirit.

2 Thessalonians 3:13-15, "And as for you, brothers, never tire of doing what is right. 14 If anyone does not obey our instruction in this letter, take special note of him. Do not associate with him, in order that he may feel ashamed. 15 Yet do not regard him as an enemy, but warn him as a brother."

It is of the *utmost* importance for His *Highest*, that the few of us who have been Blessed with sobriety and maturity in our relationship with Christ, share our good fortune with our brothers and sisters in Christ, who are less fortunate, and are still struggling in their battles with drug and alcohol addictions. The calling and need for mature mentors in this area is great. Christ's message to all of us in Matthew 28: 19-20, is perfectly clear, 19, "Go ye therefore, and teach all nations, baptizing them in the name of the Father, and of the Son, and of the Holy Ghost: 20 Teaching them to observe all things whatsoever I have commanded you: and, lo, I am with you always, even unto the end of the world. Amen."

    As mentors, we'll constantly be challenged to restore someone's Faith and trust in God, in The Gospel Truth, in the Church, and finally in themselves, for those who have either fallen away, or those who have recently accepted Christ in their lives. A good mentor's job is never finished, as once an alcoholic or an addict can consider themselves "set Free," and "recovered" from their addictions, the mentors job title is simply changed to "lifetime friend", or perhaps "disciple"! No longer receiving phone calls in the middle of the night hearing the words, "help me," but instead hearing the words, "do you know someone who *I* can help?" This is what it means to be **SAVED and SOBER!**

CHAPTER 11

Broken Hearts and Families

Drug and alcohol addictions destroy millions of families and children's lives!

The head of the household should "be above reproach",...

1 Timothy 3:2-4,
Now the overseer is to be above reproach, faithful to his wife, temperate, self-controlled, respectable, hospitable, able to teach, 3, not given to ***drunkenness****, not violent but gentle, not quarrelsome, not a lover of money. 4, He must manage his own family well and see that his children obey him, and he must do so in a manner worthy of full respect......*
Proverbs 11:29
Whoever brings ruin on their family will inherit only wind, and the fool will be servant to the wise.

Very few families today, live according to God's word in 1Timothy 3:2-4. Even in Christian families, it's beginning to be an overlooked virtue, and in *any* family where addictions have taken control, satan is ruling the roost! As long as we allow satan to rule our lives, there will be no hope for us, our families, or our children's future. Until we surrender to, and allow God to rule our lives, and guide us, our addictions will continue to cause the pain and suffering that's been tearing our families apart forever. Anyone reading this who's experienced this battle with addictions, knows exactly what I'm talking about.

Christ died on the Cross a long time ago to free us from our bondage to sin, or our addictions. All we need to do to receive that freedom, is to accept that simple Truth, repent of our sins, according to Acts 26:20, ask Jesus into our lives as our Savior, and trust and obey Him. Once we've done that, the biggest obstacle we'll encounter in our new life with Christ, will be satan, our enemy, he does not want you here! You're probably here, reading this right now, because he's been chasing after your soul with drug and alcohol abuse most of your life, and he certainly doesn't want you turning to Christ for Salvation *or* recovery from your addictions! You can count on his tricks, lies, deception, and trials in your life in an attempt to discourage you and wear you down, and turn you against God, but more importantly you can count on GOD'S Love, Grace and Power, to carry you, through your Faith of a mustard seed, (Matthew 17:20), to Victory over satan in this battle of Spiritual Warfare!

This will not be an easy task. It will require your undivided attention, vigilance, and patience. Proverbs 4:20; "My son, **pay attention** to what I say; turn your ear to my words." 1 Peter 5:8; "Be sober, **be vigilant**; because your adversary the devil, as a roaring lion, walketh about, seeking whom he may devour:" Romans 12:12; "Be joyful in hope, **patient** in affliction, faithful in prayer." The enemy will be on your heels 24/7. You must stay one step ahead of him by staying very close to God, in His Word and in prayer and in Fellowship with other Christians. Ask God for a discerning Spirit to keep you from being mislead by the many false teachers satan will send your way to try to trip you up! We can't get enough of God, His Word, and His Spirit when we're in a battle for our lives, and the lives are of our families. Satan loves to keep members in their addictions because he can destroy several people at the same

Satan is no slump! That's why we need God in our lives every minute of every day until we can declare victory! The minute we take our eyes off of God, satan will be right there waiting to distract us through temptation. With God, there is hope even in temptation, 1 Corinthians 10:13, "No temptation has overtaken you except what is common to mankind. And God is faithful; he will not let you be tempted beyond what you can bear. But when you are tempted, he will also provide a way out so that you can endure it." Again, winning the war over addictions will not be an easy task. It will require your undivided attention, vigilance, and patience. God has already proven His Love for you by sending His Son, Jesus Christ, to the Cross, to be a Sacrifice for your sins. Now, if we've been Born Again, by accepting Him as our Lord and Savior, and committed our lives to Him and His service, we must prove our Love for Him through *our* sacrifice of repentance and obedience. Acts 26:20, "First to those in Damascus, then to those in Jerusalem and in all Judea, and then to the Gentiles, I preached that they should ***repent*** and turn to God and demonstrate their repentance by their deeds." Deuteronomy 5:33, "Walk in ***obedience*** to all that the Lord your God has commanded you, so that you may live and prosper and prolong your days in the land that you will possess."

This commitment to Him should result in a Spirit of Love and desire and willingness to please our Heavenly Father. When our one desire is to please him, we should expect to see rewards and Blessings from Him, according to His will for us. Where and when many of us fail, and instead of rewards and Blessings and answers to prayers, we find ourselves in constant trials and tribulations, including the continuous curse of addictions, is when we refuse to repent and walk in obedience. The entire book of Deuteronomy is a complete illustration of this simple Truth, although by no means the only place in God's Word where we'll find instructions on repenting and obedience, and the consequences of failing to do so. Parents who Love their children will discipline them, and not reward them for their bad behavior, but punish them. We should expect no less from God. Revelation 3:19, "Those whom I love I rebuke and discipline. So be earnest and repent." Proverbs 3:11, "My child, don't reject the Lord's discipline, and don't be upset when he corrects you." Hebrews 12:7, "Endure hardship as discipline; God is treating you as his children. For what children are not disciplined by their father?"

It is totally our choice and decision as to how long we choose to wait to accept Gods Word as The Truth, and begin to obey it. As addicts, each day we wait, we submit our families and children to the consequences of our own ignorance and selfish behavior. As addicts with children, the simple reality is that when an alcoholic or an addict gets drunk or high, they're incapable of being a responsible parent. The minute a parent gets drunk or stoned, they become mentally impaired at best, or completely unconscious, which leads to the abandonment and neglect of their children, which is nothing less than child abuse and endangerment. The very act of becoming intoxicated or high on drugs, any drugs, renders one first, disoriented and confused, then often resulting in complete unconsciousness. Drug and alcohol abuse destroys all sense of reality, and the longer someone stays in this mentally impaired state of mind, the more likely they are to become permanently impaired. You cannot and should not consider yourself capable, or worthy of accepting the responsibilities of safely or effectively raising a child as long as you continue entangled in the bondage of addictions. Children need the security of two sober, loving and caring parents, a mother and a father, who's number one priority and concern and devotion is the health, welfare, and future of their children. Anything less is contributing to the neglect of the child's best interests.

Families can't possibly survive the pain, suffering, turmoil, and complete dysfunction that accompanies addictions. Even if only one parent is an addict, the stress it puts on the other is usually intolerable, and will almost always lead to divorce. The longer the one sober spouse endures, the children will always be the silent victims, suffering unimaginable damage. The most significant damage being insecurity, and the many related effects that insecurity produces. The first effect usually being the child turning to drugs and or alcohol themselves, following in the parents footsteps. A child typically, clings to the parents, and sees their behavior as normal. Unless there's some outside intervention or at least one parent who's clean and sober, or an older sibling who's capable of taking responsibility for the younger sibling, a child whose parents are addicts has little chance to survive these brutal circumstances. Insecurity breeds hopelessness, and hopelessness feeds insecurity, a vicious cycle that's deeply rooted in almost every home that's been overtaken by addictions.

As I've said throughout this book, alcoholics and addicts are masters of deception, when you add this along with denial, a helpless, voiceless, abandoned and neglected child may spend their entire childhood in an environment unfit for an animal. Because of the deception and denial, a situation like this may go on for years without anyone knowing there's a problem. If the parents won't admit there's a problem with themselves, they certainly won't see any problems in their children. All too often we don't discover the problem until it's too late and one of these children ends up on the evening news, having reached a breaking point and committed some great tragedy. Our news has been filled with these stories recently, but rarely is the truth of the background events revealed. No matter how violent or heinous the incident might have been, the child perpetrator is always described by those who knew him as "a nice boy," or "our son would never do such a thing," or "I had no idea he was so disturbed."

Years ago there was a cliché traveling around for some time, that whenever a child displayed some negative behavior in a public place, the comment would be made, "some peoples kids"! When I first heard this, I said "no, you have it backwards, it should be, some kids parents"! It is always the parent's responsibility to raise their children. Period! No matter how challenging a child might be, the parent is responsible for the child's welfare and future. It is a great tragedy and irresponsibility for parents with addictions to abuse their innocent and defenseless children through neglect and abandonment! I suspect that if parents were held totally responsible for their children's actions until they were 21, no matter the circumstances, that many parents would change their behavior and become the parents God intended them to be, loving, caring, and concerned. Even if a child runs away from home and kills someone, the parents should still go on trial as accomplices, because they are! It was their failed responsibility that led the child to run away in the first place.

I know that very few parents will agree with me, because we've turned into a society of irresponsibility. Every negative, evil action or event that takes place in the world today is always someone else's fault. It is a natural instinct to blame someone else for everything that goes wrong in our lives, that stems from our sinful nature of pride. No parent will admit that they've failed miserably in the most important job they've been given, raising children. No matter what the circumstances, or how obvious their fault may be, they'll always blame it on someone or something else. If parents took their job of parenting, and the responsibly that goes with it seriously, they would make the necessary changes in their lives to ensure their children's welfare and future.

In homes where the parents are alcoholics or addicts, the first obstacle to overcome is the denial that they have a problem with drug and alcohol use. Denial of drug and alcohol use and abuse is also caused by pride. Unfortunately, since pride is sin, without God in a person's life and the knowledge of His Word, an alcoholic or addict might spend years, or a lifetime in denial. Here we have a situation where our society is partially at fault. In secular recovery programs such as AA, the discussion of sin or anything to do with Christianity is forbidden, in fact "drunkenness" is considered a disease rather than sin, so the Truth of pride being a sin is never discussed. They may agree that pride is part of the denial factor, but they really have no way of dealing with it other than "wishing" it would go away. The same is true with their thinking that they have a disease, all they can do is "wish" someone will come along with a pill to "cure" them.

Christians, on the other hand "***should***" know that pride and "drunkenness" are sins, and that when we become born again we receive the power of the Holy Spirit, (Acts 1:8), which empowers us to repent of our sins. The emphasis on "should" is because many Christians in addiction recovery today don't understand this simple Truth. The reason being that most Churches have been using secular 12-step recovery programs to counsel their members, rather than scripture from the Gospel. Scripture, The Truth, will set captives free, (Isaiah 42:7, 61:1-2, John 8:32,), secular hogwash will not! Secular hogwash will only keep one in bondage. And yet millions of God fearing Christians have been fed secular hogwash in so-called Christian 12-step addiction recovery programs that begin in step #1 with the words, "you are powerless"! Here, because it's in Church, it's not just hogwash, but pure blasphemy!

    Until pastors wake up and smell the coffee, examine the lives of the men and women struggling with The Truth, and how to apply it in their lives, these sheep will never be "set free from the bondage of sin." I have encountered hundreds of men and women over the past 2 decades, addicts, inmates, and homosexuals, who defend and justify their sinful behavior and lifestyles with the words, "we're all sinners" taken from a complete misunderstanding of *"out of context"* scripture such as 1 John 1:8-10, or from Paul's words in Romans 7:14-20. They've been led to believe Gods Grace is a license to continue in their sinful ways. This misunderstanding is a death sentence to alcoholics and addicts and their families whose only hope is in the Cross of Christ, and the Truth, which will set them free, ***"IF,"*** they follow God's will and purpose for their life as He teaches throughout His Word, so that they can be **SAVED and SOBER!**

CHAPTER 12

Child Abandonment and Abuse!

Proverbs 22:6 KJV
Train up a child in the way he should go: and when he is old, he will not depart from it.
Deuteronomy 6:7
And thou shalt teach them diligently unto thy children, and shalt talk of them when thou sittest in thine house, and when thou walkest by the way, and when thou liest down, and when thou risest up.
Proverbs 14:26
Whoever fears the Lord has a secure fortress, and for their children it will be a refuge.
Proverbs 20:7
The righteous lead blameless lives; blessed are their children after them.
Proverbs 22:6 NIV
Start children off on the way they should go, and even when they are old they will not turn from it.
Ephesians 6:4,
And, ye fathers, provoke not your children to wrath: but bring them up in the nurture and admonition of the Lord.
Colossians 3:21,
Fathers, provoke not your children to anger, lest they be discouraged.
1 Timothy 3:4
He must manage his own family well and see that his children obey him, and he must do so in a manner worthy of full respect.
Titus 1:6

An elder must be blameless, faithful to his wife, a man whose children believe and are not open to the charge of being wild and disobedient.

According to scripture and a little common sense, we should be able to see that *any* drug addict or alcoholic, who happens to be a parent raising a child, is guilty of abandoning and neglecting that child whenever they are under the influence of their drugs of choice. Furthermore, abandoning and neglecting a child is a form of child abuse.

Some time ago, when I was still raising my children, a cliché came along that said, ***"some parents' kids!"*** When there were children around who were acting up or out of control. This quote had gone viral, long before "viral" existed, and seemed to pin the blame of children's poor behavior on the children, as if it was their fault that they were acting up. A great opportunity for the parents to deny any responsibility for their failure in raising their children. The first time I heard this comment, I immediately corrected the individual, and explained that it's the parents' responsibility to raise their children, not the other way around. Of course it wasn't received well, as the parent immediately recoiled into denial as most parents will do when confronted about their out-of-control children's behavior. Usually when we see children who are "out of control," it's because the ***parents*** are "out of control"! Perhaps, not disciplining their children properly, because they weren't disciplined themselves properly when they were growing up. Whatever the reason, rarely will we find parents who are willing to take the responsibility for being the cause of their children's misbehavior. Frequently they'll blame the school system and teachers, or babysitters, or other family members, or genes, and almost always will be in total denial, first, that their child has a problem, and second, that they've had anything to do with the cause of the problem. They'll have lots of invalid reasons and excuses why it's not their fault, it's quite common for a parent first, to blame the other parent, then the school, and if those excuses don't work, then they'll blame God. It's always someone else's fault, but never theirs.

I've heard at least a million times, a parent blaming "sugar" as the reason for their child's climbing the walls, but ***who*** gave them the "sugar"? Of course there are many occasions when there *are* a number of valid reasons, both mental and physical circumstances that are beyond the parents control, that cause children to misbehave. But I would suggest that in our society today, most of the circumstances could be avoided if the parents were more responsible, loving, caring, concerned, and most importantly, <u>***involved***</u> in their child's life! Far too many parents are completely disconnected from their children's lives. They falsely claim to be too busy, when a closer evaluation would reveal the truth to be selfishness, laziness, a lack of caring, or a complete lack of understanding the responsibility involved in raising a child, especially in the dark world in which we live today.

A child needs to be shown that there is a beautiful, bright, colorful, and happy world they can choose to live in, and not just the dark and ugly one that's portrayed in our news today and on TV. One of the reasons we have so many children growing up in the dark, ugly, and violent world, is that there are far too many parents who abandon and neglect their children by turning the TV or video games into a full-time babysitter. This is not something new, and in fact has been going on for decades, and I would propose has a great deal to do with the dark, ugly, and violent world we see emerging around us these days. I'm speaking particularly of the many children we see turning into mass murderers, violent criminals, and drug dealers who are filling up our prisons today.

There's no doubt in my mind that the biggest reason we see this moral decline in our society is the absence of parents in our children's lives. Whether they're missing physically, because they're workaholics, placing more value on their material lifestyles than their children's welfare, or they're missing emotionally and mentally because they're in a drug induced coma from drug and alcohol use and abuse, their intentional absence is nothing less than abandonment, which is a form of child abuse.

I suspect that 99% of the parents who fit the above categories, will deny this allegation with a variety of expletives. The truth is very painful and this particular one perhaps excruciating and unbearable. Rarely, if ever in my 30 years in recovery has this conversation ever come up for debate. I'm sure fist-fights and brawls would have broken out in most of the 12-step meetings I ever attended if someone accused another of child abuse! Again, the truth is very painful and people just "can't handle the truth"!

This book is all about the Truth, as in God's Truth, and while there's no mention in the bible about child abandonment or abuse, it only takes common sense to realize that when a parent is absent from their child's life, by being mentally impaired from the use and abuse of drugs and alcohol, they're absent, and guilty not only of abandonment and abuse, but of endangerment as well! When a person gets excessively wasted on drugs and alcohol, the house could burn down around them without them ever waking up! How can I make such a brazen statement? I'll be the first to admit that I'm guilty myself of having "been there and done that." My wife and I were both drunks and addicts during the early years of our children's lives.

Fortunately, by the Grace of God, He delivered me from the nightmare of addictions. Unfortunately, it took a divorce to do so. But that gave my children an opportunity to see over the next few years two different lifestyles of living, mine, which was clean and sober, or their moms, who remarried another drunk, and continued living trapped in addictions until they killed her a few years later. My children, Praise God, were able to make a conscious choice to follow my example of living clean and sober, and are both drug and alcohol free today, 30 years later. Am I qualified or experienced enough to make the above accusations with a clear conscience? Absolutely! And I'll spell it out again for those who might not understand. *Any* drug addict or alcoholic, who happens to be a parent raising a child, is guilty of abandoning and neglecting that child whenever they are under the influence of their drugs of choice. Furthermore, abandoning and neglecting a child is a form of child abuse. Period, end of debate.

Now, about denial. Denial is not the answer. It's just an invalid excuse that people use to dispel their responsibility for any negative behavior of their own, or that their children might display. It's not a word just used regarding drug and alcohol addictions. It's a psychological reaction used to hide from the reality of any unacceptable bad behavior and poor choices in life, as well as an escape mechanism to hide from life's many painful experiences, as well as the Truth. Most people who use drugs and alcohol, do so to escape reality, then by the time they discover that it doesn't work, they've become addicted to them, and they turn to denial to escape from that additional reality. People simply can't face the truth or reality, and sometimes spend their entire lives in denial and hiding from various truths and realities of life's many trials. It's as common as the cold.

This chapter is about child abandonment,

neglect, and abuse. Because drugs and alcohol play such a big role in that topic, and denial plays such a big role in drug and alcohol use and abuse, there's another chapter dedicated to that topic.

Today, we're living in a culture where there is widespread child abuse and neglect that includes everything from the most heinous and unimaginable physical and sexual violence and exploitation, to a more common and subtle abuse, such as neglect and abandonment, all of which shatters and destroys a child's innocence, leaving deep emotional scars, many of which may never heal. Millions of parents today ignore their children for a variety of invalid reasons that they come up with. The fact and truth is, *any* excuse is invalid! Often, our society itself is partially to blame for a number of reasons, one, being the economy, which has impoverished millions of families and caused the husband and wife both to work 2 jobs just to keep food on the table. The end result being that their children often grow up as orphans. In many of these cases the parents really don't have any options or choices because the alternatives would force them to be homeless.

There are millions of other parents who live in less than favorable economic conditions who manage to raise their children successfully because they prioritize the time and attention they spend with their children. There are many other cases however, where the parents have lots of other alternatives and choices, but because of drug and alcohol addictions, and the accompanying dysfunctional behavior, they're incapable of raising a normal family. They can't take care of themselves, let alone a child.

It's not our children's responsibility, and certainly not *God's fault,* that our children are out of control, when they are. It's *our* responsibility to raise our children from the day they are born, until they move from our homes, and to teach *them* responsibility, as well as right from wrong, obedience, and honesty. It's our responsibility to teach them to walk, talk, and tie their shoes, brush their teeth, and comb their hair, to prepare them for college, and to raise their own families. If we don't show them how to do all these things and thousands of other things, who will? Child care, babysitters, and nannies can never replace loving, caring, concerned, and responsible parents.

As Christian parents, our biggest responsibility is to lead our children to God as soon as possible. (Deut.6:1-9) Then to show them the importance of letting God take over *their* lives and teach them how to grow and mature in *His* ways for them. With His guidance, and *His* Wisdom and instruction, taught through us, our children should **not** grow up "out of control." I've carefully chosen the words "should not", because we never know what God's plan is for our lives, or our children's. He knows when *we or* our children might need some "refining," according to His Will and plan for us. We must teach our children the importance of Faith and obedience to get us through this process of refining and trials. As Christians, we should recognize and pass on to our children that this is how we grow and mature with the Lord.

As Christian parents who are in addiction recovery, who are raising children, we'll require some very "special" attention and help from God, we'll require much "refining", and instruction from God through answered prayer. We'll first need to develop our own Faith, and conquer our battles with satan over our addictions before we can begin to be an accountable and responsible parent. Once we've moved beyond denial, and experienced a little bit of sobriety, we'll begin to recognize the pain and suffering we've caused our children and spouses. If we don't believe we *have,* then we're still in denial!

When we're ready to accept this painful truth, and take full responsibility for the damage we've already done to our children, families, friends, and others, we'll be ready to begin to move forward in our recovery, and in the job of being a responsible parent. Until we reach this point, we'll be nothing more than an absent, irresponsible parent, guilty of the charge of child abuse by reason of neglect and abandonment. Don't try to deny and hide from that very painful truth, but face it, and change it! The choice is yours, and you only get one chance at raising your children.

Often much of the damage we've done is not easily recognized. Not only have we been in denial, but often some of our loved ones may be in denial as well. Often our children and spouses over a period of time, begin to think that the dysfunction in their home is normal. One major element of our families' involvement in our addiction that we may not fully recognize, or understand is abandonment. How every time we use drugs or alcohol to "escape" from the reality of this evil and destructive world we're living in, or the pain and suffering from a past experience that we're trying to hide from, we're also hiding from, and abandoning our children and loved ones. They might not know who we are, even if we're sitting next to them in the same room for years, if we're drunk or high, we might as well be a million miles away! This could be the biggest tragedy of drug and alcohol addiction. There is not one person, who now or ever, has been addicted to drugs or alcohol, who hasn't negatively affected or impacted someone else. Usually it's our family and our children. The minute we get drunk or stoned we become mentally paralyzed and unconscious. The more often we engage in this behavior, the more long term damage we do both to ourselves and our loved ones.

Another very common, but often unrecognized

element of addictions, particularly while the addict is still in denial, is enablement. Many spouses and family members, and friends will unintentionally enable their loved ones with addictions simply by allowing it to happen. By ignoring that there's a problem, or denying that there is a problem, by turning a blind eye to it, by turning the other cheek when there's been abuse, by not holding their loved ones accountable and responsible in the beginning, is all a form of enabling. By not demanding change or repentance of the loved one who's hurting them, as well as themselves, is a form of enabling. Often the children in these circumstances become the "hidden" or "silent" enabler. One spouse will put up with, often for years, with the other spouses addictive behavior and subsequent abuse, thinking that they're protecting the child. Not realizing the emotional damage that the child is suffering, and its long-term effects. When a loved one is hurting us or subjecting us to any type of pain, and or suffering, because of their addictive behavior, we have every right to step in and demand an apology and a promise to change. The sooner we learn to do this, the many more years of pain and suffering we'll save ourselves and our loved ones from. The longer we allow it to continue, the more difficult it will be for our loved one to change and find victory over the bondage of addiction.

 And still another often unrecognized or overlooked element of addictions that destroys our families and affects millions of innocent children is imprisonment. Our prisons are filled today to overflowing capacity with people who are there because of drugs and alcohol. While there seems to be no absolutely reliable or official numbers on how many of those incarcerated in jails and prisons at any given time are there because of drugs and alcohol, it seems a fairly common number used is 70-80% of the total populations. In addiction recovery programs, a very common term and conversation is about "relapse." In prisons, a similar word is "recidivism," which refers to those who get out, only to return usually within a short period of time, and that statistic is also in the 70-80% range. The frightening statistic here is that in both cases the common denominator for the reason of incarceration *or* re-incarceration, is always the abuse of drugs and alcohol. These crimes range from stealing a six pack of beer from the local grocery store, to drug dealing murders, from robbing a bank to support a drug habit, to habitual D.U.I.'s, leading to a drunk-driving accident that kills an innocent child or family. The news is filled with these stories every day, but rarely if ever do they report on the root cause. That drug and alcohol addiction is out of control in this country. When parents are in prison, they've abandoned their children and families and begin this vicious cycle over again. The billion dollar secular addiction recovery industry can't fix it. The billion dollar judicial and penal system can't fix it, the government's attempts have all failed. It *is*, and has always been out of control for years, and *man* can't fix it. Only God can fix it, and we as Christians need to start trusting God to take control of our lives, which He has been anyways. We need to surrender fully, and quit resisting His plan for us, which does not include our wasting our lives addicted to drugs and alcohol.

 Many of these men and women in prisons are parents, who, if their addictions didn't end up breaking up the home and family, their incarceration probably did, or certainly will at some point, if they don't repent and change directions. Rarely, will a spouse stay with someone who is incarcerated. If addictions were involved, which is usually the case, it's often an opportunity, even a "golden opportunity" for the "free" spouse to get away from the other. Nonetheless, the end result is another broken family with children being abandoned by one parent or the other. If the child is old enough to have gained the trust, and developed a relationship with the incarcerated parent, the abandonment will be seen as betrayal, which will produce disrespect, distrust, and resentment towards that parent, or both parents. It's not uncommon for troubled youth to blame both parents. The second one for allowing the first one to get away with their dysfunctional behavior. No matter what the abuse, the child will blame the non-abuser for allowing the abuser to get away with it. And perhaps rightfully so in most cases. Either parent is always responsible for the others actions and behavior, just as they both are for their children's actions and behavior. The emotional damage will leave deep scars, and fester into insecurity that can have disastrous long-ranging results.

Insecurity may contribute to, and encourage compensatory behaviors such as alcohol or drug addictions or other escape mechanisms such as the development of shyness, paranoia and social withdrawal, and depression. Many will turn to varying sexual dysfunctions, such as pornography, homosexual behavior, or promiscuity. I've noticed for years that with every homosexual person I've ever met, it seems that their insecurity stands out like a flashing neon sign, many of them seem to communicate among themselves like 5 year old children. They seem to either fear conversation, and refuse to look a person in the eyes. Or they boastfully exploit their sinful behavior and lifestyle. These are all signs of insecurity. Hence, the closet, which they're either in, or out of, depending on the mood of the moment. Moody people are insecure people not knowing who they are from one minute to the next. Alcoholics and addicts tend to follow these traits as well. The above symptoms are all very common in 12-step addiction recovery meetings, especially noticeable among those new to recovery. As people spend more time in these meetings you begin to see them become more comfortable and start shedding many of the obvious symptoms of insecurity. Insecurity becomes a vicious, endless cycle passed down from one generation to the next, which leads to hopelessness. There's an entire chapter devoted to the topic of insecurity.

Now let's go back to our children's plight that lies ahead for them if we don't change our path, and turn to God. Our biggest responsibility on this planet as a parent is the welfare, and future of our children. It's all about perspective; if we can't take care of ourselves, we certainly can't take care of our children and families. And we can't take care of ourselves, *by* ourselves. We need God in our lives to guide us and lead us through the many battles and challenges that addictions will take us through. If you don't know God, you need to. If you *do* know God, and you're still struggling with drugs or alcohol, you need to get to know Him much better. Draw Him so close to you (James 4:8), that you can whisper to each other in prayer. In this noisy, chaotic world we live in, we need to find a quiet place to develop a very close, personal relationship with our Lord and Savior. May we hear His every breath. Psalm 17:6, "I call on you, my God, for you will answer me; turn your ear to me and hear my prayer."

If we want to be the best parents we can be, we must *lead* our children to God, then to teach them how to let God *lead them* for the rest of their lives. (Acts 2:39, Deut.4:9, 6:1-9,11:19, Ps.78:5, Joel 1:3) We can't accomplish this until we've completely surrendered *our* lives to Him, and are letting *Him lead* us. *Complete* surrender is vital! Many Christians want to hold onto as much of the world as possible, for as long as possible. Until God shows them what it means to "pick up the Cross and follow Him." They want to be "Cultural Christians", (Patrick Morley) they want to "accept Christ, without forsaking the world", (A.W.Tozer) God's Word says to "Repent and be Saved." (Acts 3:19) We want our cake and eat it too. We want to be saved, but not have to repent and give up our sinful behavior. If we want to be the best *parents* we can be for our children, we need to start being the best Christians we can be for God. We need to be "My Utmost For His Highest". (Oswald Chambers)

As Christians in addiction recovery, it's difficult to give "My Utmost For His Highest," when we're using drugs and alcohol to escape from reality. Many will be struggling with issues of insecurity, which breeds low self-esteem, guilt, fear, and unforgiveness. We're all sinners, (1 John 1: 8-9) and if we haven't learned to accept God's forgiveness, and then to forgive ourselves, we'll not have the peace we need to be good parents. To be the best parents we can be, we need the inner peace that only comes from a close personal relationship with God. Do you want to be the *best* parent you can be, or are you willing to settle for second best? Only God can help you be the best parent you can be. Are your children worth making that decision for today? Don't wait until tomorrow. (Acts 2:39, Deut.4:9, 6:1-9, 11:19, Ps.78:5, Joel 1:3). The next time you see or hear someone make the comment, "Some people's kids", let them know they've got it backwards! Our children have little control over how the parents and the world raise them. They learn and follow according to example, and if they spend enough time in a dysfunctional environment, they begin to see the dysfunctions as normal.

Children are very resilient and learn to hide their fears and pain. But only on the surface, the scars are deep and can't be seen, but eventually the damage will be exposed, as we grow older it will begin to come to the surface. Our pasts will always have some impact on our present and future lives. There's no way to eliminate our memories, only by the Grace of God can we learn to live with them, and hopefully learn from them. Hopefully we've matured enough to deal with them. But for many, no matter how mature we may be, or think we are, dealing with the past in a way that won't affect the present or the future can be a very difficult task. I believe that even the strongest survivors of childhood neglect, abandonment, and abuse will always harbor certain painful memories. Memories that will be awakened from time to time, and bring us back to a dark time and place in our lives, that we would prefer to stay away from. What we can't afford to do, is linger there for any degree of time. A quick visit, and a quick return to the reality of the present time won't cause any damage, but for those who linger in, and dwell on the past, we will eventually start living it all over again. If we stay there long enough, the pain will return, and we'll start looking for ways to hide or kill the pain. Perhaps using the same "painkillers," or escape mechanisms that our parents used. And then the cycle begins all over again.

There's only one way to break this vicious, destructive cycle. It's to drop to our knees and surrender to God! Ask His Son, Jesus into our lives to lead us. To repent and ask God for forgiveness of our sins. To declare Jesus as our Lord and Savior and through Faith, believe that He will provide us with the power and strength to turn from our old wicked and sinful behavior, so that we can be **SAVED and SOBER!**

CHAPTER 13

A Bible Study on Faith and Salvation For Those in Addiction Recovery

Are we letting satan control are Recovery? Or are we Confident about Our Conversion And God's Word and promises?

If we're **SAVED and SOBER**, we are brand new, (2 Corinthians 5:17, "Therefore if any man be in Christ, he is a new creature: old things are passed away; behold, all things are become new.") We should, with the Faith of a mustard seed have full confidence and assurance of our Salvation and freedom from the bondage of addictions according to,...

Ephesians 3:12,
*In him and through faith in him we may approach God with freedom and **confidence.***
Hebrews 3:6,
*But Christ is faithful as the Son over God's house. And we are his house, if indeed we hold firmly to our **confidence** and the hope in which we glory.*
Hebrews 4:16,
*Let us then approach God's throne of grace with **confidence**, so that we may receive mercy and find grace to help us in our time of need.*
Hebrews 10:35,

*So do not throw away your **confidence**; it will be richly rewarded.*
Hebrews 11:1,
*[Faith in Action] Now faith is **confidence** in what we hope for and **assurance** about what we do not see.*
Hebrews 13:6,
*So we say with **confidence**, "The Lord is my helper; I will not be afraid. What can mere mortals do to me?"*
1 John 5:14,
*This is the **confidence** we have in approaching God: that if we ask anything according to his will, he hears us.*
Acts 17:31,
*Because he hath appointed a day, in the which he will judge the world in righteousness by that man whom he hath ordained; whereof he hath given **assurance** unto all men, in that he hath raised him from the dead.*
Colossians 2:2,
*That their hearts might be comforted, being knit together in love, and unto all riches of the **full assurance** of understanding, to the acknowledgement of the mystery of God, and of the Father, and of Christ;*
1 Thessalonians 1:5,
*For our gospel came not unto you in word only, but also in power, and in the Holy Ghost, and in much **assurance**; as ye know what manner of men we were among you for your sake.*
Hebrews 6:11,
*And we desire that every one of you do shew the same diligence to the **full assurance** of hope unto the end:*
Hebrews 10:22,
*Let us draw near with a true heart in **full assurance** of faith, having our hearts sprinkled from an evil conscience, and our bodies washed with pure water.*

When we continue to allow satan to control our sinful behavior, we're not only displaying our lack of Faith and assurance, but in essence we're calling God a liar. If we are to stand firm against Satan's attacks and deception, it is important that we clear up any misunderstanding we might have regarding our Faith and Salvation. As Christians in addiction recovery we must recognize that it's the devils job to tear down our confidence and assurance. So we must know and stand strong on the scripture that proves him to be a liar. We must know and understand God's Truth in all areas of our lives, and as it applies especially to our addiction recovery. Secular addiction recovery programs have no place in our Churches, yet are found and practiced in far too many of them. The only thing a Church should be teaching a Christian is God's Word, and ***never*** man's philosophy, (Col. 2:8), "See to it that no one takes you captive through hollow and deceptive philosophy, which depends on human tradition and the elemental spiritual forces of this world rather than on Christ."

The only way to grow in Spiritual Fullness in Christ, is through scripture. It is vital to our recovery that we continue to grow and mature in Christ daily. (Hebrews 5:13) Picking up our cross, (Luke 9:23), and following Christ on the narrow road, (Matthew 7:14) is a lifetime journey and commitment. Once we've taken the first step of our recovery, being born again, (John 3:3), that's the "new beginning," we've become a brand new person, (2 Cor. 5:17) on a brand new journey, seeking and following God's plan for us, rather than following the old man satan who used to lead us on our old path to destruction!

Spiritual Fullness in Christ

Colossians 2:5-14,
*5, For though I am absent from you in body, I am present with you in spirit and delight to see how disciplined you are and how firm your **faith** in Christ is.*

How ***disciplined*** are you, and how firm are you in your **Faith**? Many who still struggle with their addictions, do so from lack of discipline, Job 36:10, *"He openeth also their ear to discipline, and commandeth that they return from iniquity,"* or are you one of little **Faith**, Matthew 17:20, *Jesus replied, "Because you have so little **faith**. Truly I tell you, if you have **faith** as small as a mustard seed, you can say to this mountain, 'Move from here to there,' and it will move. Nothing will be impossible for you."*

It is through **Faith** that we are saved, and it will be through **Faith** that we find recovery, and become Saved and Sober! *Ephesians 2:8, For by grace are ye saved through **faith**; and that not of yourselves: it is the gift of God:*

*Colossians 2:6-14: 6, So then, just as you received Christ Jesus as Lord, continue to live your lives in him, 7, rooted and built up in him, strengthened in the **faith** as you were taught, and overflowing with thankfulness.*

Most of us were overwhelmed with joy and peace when we were first Saved. For many of us, we immediately recognized the miracle that took place in us, that we had been changed and were made new in Christ,(2 Cor. 5:17), and we believed that we could move mountains! Many of us however, just like in our earthly marriages, the joy and excitement wears off over time. For an alcoholic or an addict, that can be fatal! We must renew our vows and commitment to Christ daily, and focus on The Cross, and how it Saved us and brought us to being recovered. We must be on our knees daily as the enemy will be trying to stay one step ahead of us, we must learn how to protect ourselves from his attacks and deception.

Col. 2:8-12, " See to it that no one takes you captive through hollow and deceptive philosophy, which depends on human tradition and the elemental spiritual forces of this world rather than on Christ. 9, For in Christ all the fullness of the Deity lives in bodily form, 10, and in Christ you have been brought to fullness. He is the head over every power and authority. 11, In him you were also circumcised with a circumcision not performed by human hands. Your whole self ruled by the flesh was put off when you were circumcised by Christ, 12, having been buried with him in baptism, in which you were also raised with him through your **faith** *in the working of God, who raised him from the dead."*

Have you been brought to fullness through total surrender to His power and authority? Have you put off and buried your old self that was ruled by the flesh? Have you been raised with Him through your **Faith** in the working of God, who raised Him from the dead? Have you accepted your Salvation and have the **confidence** that God has made you alive with Christ, and has forgiven all your sins and nailed them to the cross?

13, When you were dead in your sins and in the uncircumcision of your flesh, God made you alive with Christ. He forgave us all our sins, 14 having canceled the charge of our legal indebtedness, which stood against us and condemned us; he has taken it away, nailing it to the cross.

Alcoholics and addicts in the flesh without Jesus, have no power to defeat addictions, or satan, the enemy, the ruler over all sin. Christians, on the other hand have all the necessary power to defeat satan and overcome addictions according to Jesus own words in Acts 1:8, *"But ye shall receive power, after that the Holy Ghost is come upon you: and ye shall be witnesses unto me both in Jerusalem, and in all Judaea, and in Samaria, and unto the uttermost part of the earth."* And in Luke 10:19, "Behold, I give unto you power to tread on serpents and scorpions, and over all the power of the enemy: and nothing shall by any means hurt you." In Matthew 19:26 Jesus said, *"With man this is impossible, but with God all things are possible."*

As born again Christians, with the **Faith** of a mustard seed, and the **confidence** and **assurance** that God has promised us, we need to stop following mans, (or satans) lies that we've grown so accustomed to in secular 12-step addiction recovery programs, that tell us that we are "powerless." In the Christian Church that statement is pure blasphemy, contradicting the Gospel of Jesus, and a Christian should quickly flee, (1 Timothy 6:11, "But you, man of God, flee from all this, and pursue righteousness, godliness, faith, love, endurance and gentleness.") As our Faith grows with every victory over battles with the devil, building our confidence and assurance in our Salvation we find we can live **SAVED and SOBER!**

CHAPTER 14

Are you ready for change?

(1 Samuel 10:6)
"The Spirit of the Lord will come upon you in power, and you will prophesy with them; and you will be changed into a different person."
2 Corinthians 5:17
Therefore if any man be in Christ, he is a new creature: old things are passed away; behold, all things are become new.

The fear of change can be paralyzing!

Isaiah 41:10, "So do not fear, for I am with you; do not be dismayed, for I am your God.
I will strengthen you and help you;
I will uphold you with my righteous right hand."
"Fear Not"! God says again in Isaiah 43:1

Many people struggle with addiction recovery and relapse over and over because they fear change. They fear the unknown. They fear God because they don't know Him, and they've been told that He will change them, and even though they're painfully longing for change, they're terrified of the unknown. For many of us we've grown up hearing and believing all kinds of lies that we're just a useless loser who will never amount to anything in life. We've grown up in darkness and despair without ever experiencing real Love, and the simple thought of a complete change from that kind of darkness brings a fear unlike any we've ever experienced. Growing up in the dark world of drug and alcohol use and abuse, poverty, violence, childhood abandonment and abuse, renders one totally insecure and terrified of change. Change is a choice that only we get to make. No one can do it for us, and it requires making a decision. Something most alcoholics and addicts have trouble doing after years of drug and alcohol use and abuse, and the dysfunctional thinking that results. For years most of our decisions have led to disastrous consequences, and again, the fear of the unknown paralyzes us. For many of us decisions were all about responsibility, and out of fear we would choose to get drunk or high rather than make a responsible decision. Fear of failure, along with responsibility are often two of the things that leads many to drug and alcohol use in the first place.

Yet deep down inside, you know you need to change, and you desperately want to. You're tired and worn out from years of drug and alcohol use and abuse, years of pain and suffering and chaos, the loss of friends and family, jobs, health, and anything of any value, maybe you've spent far too much time in jails and prison, or on the run to avoid it, you know it's time to change if you're to live to see another day. Yet change seems like an impossible dream that only happens for others. Overcoming the fear to change takes courage. For Christians, it takes Faith to overcome that fear. And Christians are encouraged throughout God's Word to "Fear Not"! Luke 12:32, "Fear not, little flock; for it is your Father's good pleasure to give you the kingdom."

All of us who have been in this war with addictions can relate to the fear of change. We've all heard hundreds of times the lie that we need to hit bottom before we can start the process of recovery. The truth is many of us hit what we think is bottom over and over again, only to discover it was an imaginary bottom. And far too many end up dying long before they reach that imaginary bottom! The truth is that we have no idea what our bottom is, only God knows. We need to seek God and reach out to Him long before we get to our bottom, or we'll not see it either. The bottom is death! And then hell, if we haven't turned to, and surrendered to God before it's too late!

Turning to, and surrendering our lives and addictions to God, is the change we must make *before* we hit bottom. It's the only change we can make to prevent hitting bottom, and it guarantees us Eternal Life! Once we've accepted His invitation and surrendered our lives and wills to Him and His Son, Jesus Christ, who died on the Cross for our sin and addictions, once we've repented and confessed Jesus as our Lord, and put our Faith and trust in Him, we will be changed, and changed forever! (1 Samuel 10:6) "The Spirit of the Lord will come upon you in power, and you will prophesy with them; and you will *be changed* into a different person." A change that extinguishes all fear, and empowers us with the power of God, (Acts 1:8), which enables us to overcome the attacks of the enemy, turns the darkness of the world into light and Glory. With the Faith of a mustard seed, (Math. 17:20), and our obedience to Him and His will for us, we can experience these Blessings and "be set free," (John 8:31-36) from our old selves, and "be made new in Christ."(2 Cor. 5:17)

The longer we put off making this choice, the deeper we sink towards the bottom, and our lives slowly drift away from reality and become more unmanageable and dysfunctional. Our ability to make rational, intelligent, and important decisions becomes impaired and eventually impossible. The longer we wait to decide to change, the less likely we are to ever make that choice on our own, short of a miracle. God does still perform those miracles every day, but He would prefer that we make the decision ourselves without needing a miracle.

He would prefer that before we hit bottom, we would come to our senses and realize all the damage and destruction we've done in the past, and are still doing to ourselves and everyone around us. Over the years I've witnessed hundreds of my addicted friends and colleagues', including myself, damage and destroy our families and other relationships because of our addictions to drugs and alcohol and other sin. A common and true saying in addiction recovery meetings is that we "don't build relationships, but take hostages"! For many of us we've chosen to live this way for years, rather than face and overcome the fear of change. The longer we put off making that change, the more carnage we'll leave behind us. And the longer it will take to restore some of the relationships and damage. Some of the relationships may never be salvaged.

The longer we stay lost in our addictions, the deeper the hole gets that we're trying to dig our way out of. The higher we allow the walls of denial to become, the more convinced we become that we don't have a problem, but that the rest of the world around us is the problem. We keep feeding our insecurity and false security until we're paralyzed and void of any reality. Our lives eventually become so dysfunctional, that normal for us, is seen as insanity to everyone else around us. Alleys or dumpsters or a friends basement become our new homes when we're not in jail. Our friends and family have all left us and won't even answer our calls. Pawn shops become our banks to loan us a few bucks for some junk we either just stole, or found in a dumpster, and dumpsters become our kitchens.

Far, Far, Far too many have decided long before getting to this "bottom," that life in prison would be a better alternative, and there they sit. Rather than face the fear of change. Paralyzed, trembling in the shadows of the darkness of the unknown, waiting,…waiting for someone like you or I to come along and share the Good News with them! All they need to hear at this point in their lives is The Good News of God! That there is Light to end their darkness. Many of these millions of men and women, believe it or not, have never been encouraged with the Light of God's Word. They've spent lifetimes locked in the darkness of their addictions. They've spent day after day, year after year, after growing up in dark, evil, childhoods, hanging out in dark evil bars drinking, or in an alley shooting up. An environment void of very many of Gods servants sharing The Good News! In Luke 10: 2-3, He tells us, "The harvest is plentiful, but the workers are few. Ask the Lord of the harvest, therefore, to send out workers into his harvest field. 3, Go! I am sending you out like lambs among wolves.

    If you're a Christian reading this, especially one who's been set free from addictions, you must already know that the harvest is plentiful in the many meeting rooms of addiction recovery. There must be millions of Christian men and women today worldwide, in various recovery programs, who have conquered the battle over denial, only to end up in another battle over finding Gods Truth in their recovery. They've spent years fighting denial, and finally, after overcoming it and admitting that they need Jesus in their life, they end up in meeting rooms in churches, where they're not being taught Gods Truth from His Word, but instead, being taught secular principals and philosophy from a secular 12-step recovery program. They've found themselves in the new age and new world church where the "feel good" and "name it and claim it" prosperity false gospel is being taught, and the best these churches can do to counsel, minister, or teach their members who are suffering from addictions to drug, alcohol, and other sin, is to offer them non-biblical physco-babble from some secular 12-step program. A program full of blasphemy starting with step #1, where you're told that you're powerless, which is a direct contradiction to Jesus' words in Acts 1:8,... "But ye shall receive power, after that the Holy Ghost is come upon you: and ye shall be witnesses unto me both in Jerusalem, and in all Judaea, and in Samaria, and unto the uttermost part of the earth."

While there may be a huge harvest field in the world today, there may be another one right in your own church! If your church has an addiction recovery program, you might want to see what's being taught. If you're a born again believer you are not "*powerless.*" The scripture is perfectly clear; the message in 12-step addiction recovery programs led by men is not. You must learn to be like a Berean, Acts 17:11, and search the scripture daily to see if what you're being taught is God's Truth.

If you're tired and worn out from the drugs and booze and chaos, waking up in a strangers bed, or a gutter, or a jail, and you've decided it's time to change the road your on, trust this, God is good! He is not evil, he will not hurt you, He Loves you and wants the best for you. It is foolish, even insane to continue on the same path you've been on when there's a simple answer and solution. You have to make the decision, no one can do it for you. My guess is that you already know what the decision needs to be, or what it should be, but fear of the unknown is keeping you from making what you already know in your Heart is the right choice. The truth is, it's *not* an *unknown* choice, millions of others before you have chosen to accept God in their lives and have been immediately delivered from the bondage of addictions. It only seems like a mysterious, unknown place to you, simply because you've never been here. I guarantee you, once you've made this decision you will be forever grateful for God's Grace! His Amazing Grace, which is a free gift to everyone who asks Him for it, and who's willing to accept it.

    While it's a free gift, God doesn't just pass it out to everyone, we must ask for it with a repentive Heart. We must return His Love for us, by Loving Him back. That's the change we fear. We're not sure if we're capable of Loving someone else, because in our addictions we've grown accustomed to only loving ourselves out of selfishness. We're not sure if we can measure up to God's standards. The truth is we can't, and God knows it. That's why, through Grace, He sent us His Son Jesus who died on the Cross as a Sacrifice for our sin, and our inability to measure up to His standards! All we need to do to receive His Love, Grace, Forgiveness, and Blessings, is to accept this simple Truth, ask Jesus into our life and to change it, and to promise Him that we'll repent and turn from our old ways, our old sinful behavior, and turn to Him. To be Faithful and obedient, seeking His will for us and not our own.

    No matter how afraid we are of change and the unknown, this should be an easy decision for anyone who has spent any time at or near the bottom. If you're truly tired and worn out from the pain and destruction of perhaps years of addictions to drugs, booze, gambling, sex or pornography, or any other sinful behavior, and the chaos it creates in your life, and you're ready to change the road you're on, God is the answer. He's the shelter from the storm that you've been searching for, and he's waiting with open arms to receive you. Right now this very minute, without condemnation, He will welcome you no matter how hung over you might be, or un-shaven, or dirty or smelly you might be,

He wants to receive you into His family, to Save you for Eternal Fellowship with Him. He promises to make you a brand new person in 2 Corinthians 5:17, "Therefore if any man be in Christ, he is a new creature: old things are passed away; behold, all things are become new."

What does it mean to "accept Christ"? According to A.W. Tozer it means, "Bowing to Christ's Lordship" Allowing the expression "Accept Christ" to stand as an honest effort to say in short what could not be so well said any other way, let us see what we mean or should mean when we use it. To accept Christ is to form an attachment to the Person of our Lord Jesus altogether unique in human experience. The attachment is intellectual, volitional and emotional. The believer is intellectually convinced that Jesus is both Lord and Christ; he has set his will to follow Him at any cost and soon his heart is enjoying the exquisite sweetness of His fellowship. This attachment is all-inclusive in that it joyfully accepts Christ for all that He is. There is no craven division of offices whereby we may acknowledge His Saviorhood today and withhold decision on His Lordship till tomorrow. The true believer owns Christ as his All in All without reservation. He also includes all of himself, leaving no part of his being unaffected by the revolutionary transaction. Further, his attachment to Christ is all-exclusive. The Lord becomes to him not one of several rival interests, but the one exclusive attraction forever. He orbits around Christ as the earth around the sun, held in thrall by the magnetism of His love, drawing all his life and light and warmth from Him. In this happy state he is given other interests, it is true, but these are all determined by his relation to his Lord."
A.W. Tozer

In my words, we must live every minute of our lives for Christ, who Sacrificed His life for ours.

We must not only repent and be obedient and have the Faith of a mustard seed, but live our lives Sacrificially through our deeds to honor our Savior. Not works to gain Salvation, but works in honor of His sacrifice on the Cross for us. Being obedient to him out of gratitude for His grace. This is all part of the change that needs to take place in our hearts.

Another fear that many encounter that hinders their decision to change is they fear the Truth! "You can't handle the truth" became a very popular cliché in the 80's, which is still relevant today. While I don't believe Jack Nicholson was referring to God's Truth, the fact is that many can't handle God's Truth out of fear of retribution. The purpose of God's Truth is to teach us how to live our lives according to His will and righteousness. When we fail to do so and fall into sin, God's Truth will convict us, and should lead us to repentance. The problem is that many who are chained to the bondage of addictions haven't been taught this simple Truth, and spend years if not lifetimes captives to the consequences, the wrath of God, rather than His Love and Blessings. The Truth is, The Truth **WILL** "set you free," **"*If*"** you obey God, John 8:31-32, To the Jews who had believed him, Jesus said, *"If you hold to my teaching, you are really my disciples. 32, Then you will know the truth, and the truth will set you free."* Ask God *into* your heart today. Repent, and ask God to change your heart today! *("I will praise you with an upright heart as I learn your righteous laws. "*Psalm 119:7) To be born Again, and *"Therefore if any man be in Christ, he is a new creature: old things are passed away; behold, all things are become new."* (2 Corinthians 5:17) If you believe that God's Word is the Truth, you must act on it through Faith, rather than being one of little Faith, Matthew 8:26 And he saith unto them, *"Why are ye fearful, O ye of little faith? Then he arose, and rebuked the winds and the* *sea; and there was a great calm."* Let God change your heart and your life so that you can be **SAVED** and **SOBER!**

CHAPTER 15

CONCLUSION

John 8:31-32
Then said Jesus to those Jews which believed on him, If ye continue in my word, then are ye my disciples indeed; 32, And ye shall know the truth, and the truth shall make you free.

What choice do we have to end the insanity of addictions? We have the same choice we've had since the beginning of time in the garden. Just as God gave Adam and Eve directions to follow, and a choice to do so, or not, today, we have directions to follow, and the free choice to do so or not. We have the choice to follow God, or satan, to repent and turn to, and surrender our lives and wills over to The Almighty God, our Father in Heaven, and His Son Jesus Christ, and to be "set free", and **"SAVED and SOBER"**! Or not! We know right from wrong if we have any conscience at all. Our conscience is led by God's conviction, and when we ignore it we can expect to suffer the consequences. Adam and Eve experienced this Truth in the garden, and millions of us will experience it today as alcoholics and addicts who refuse to obey God's Word and His will for us. Millions of us everyday get to choose whether we'll follow satan's prompting and temptations and go down in defeat, or accept God's offer of Salvation, Redemption, and recovery, break the chains of bondage, and rise in victory! This is the only way to be set free from the bondage of addictions and sin. Thirty years ago I made the decision to accept God's offer of Salvation.

Today, I'm sharing with you in this book, what He's done for me, and taught me about His Truth, the answers that will set you free, so that you, through the Faith of a mustard seed, and His Grace, can be **SAVED** and **SOBER!**

There is only one way and one answer to conquering the battle over addictions, to winning the war with satan. That answer is surrendering our lives and wills to God, through His Son Jesus Christ! That means total, complete surrender, not partial, and not just for awhile. That means recognizing and understanding God's Word, The Truth. That every Word in the Bible is relevant in our lives. And relevant to our Salvation, as well as our recovery. It means understanding that many of God's promises regarding our Salvation and His Blessings that bring forth our recovery are conditional, and require certain actions from us. These actions are; first, repentance, then faith, then obedience, and finally claiming His promises, or having the assurance and confidence through faith, to know that He will provide what we need according to His will for us.

First, repentance, *Acts 26:20 says, "First to those in Damascus, then to those in Jerusalem and in all Judea, and then to the Gentiles, I preached that they should **repent** and turn to God and demonstrate their **repentance** by their **deeds**."* Many claim to have repented, but there is no evidence of it based on their actions. They clearly live in sin, and always have an invalid excuse to justify it.

Second, faith, *Matthew 17:20, And Jesus said unto them, "Because of your unbelief: for verily I say unto you, If ye have **faith** as a grain of mustard seed, ye shall say unto this mountain, Remove hence to yonder place; and it shall remove; and nothing shall be impossible unto you."* Many claim to have faith, but there is no evidence of it in their actions.

They live in constant fear and doubt, and are quick to ask others to pray for them when they catch a cold or have a flat tire.

Third, obedience, in *"Deuteronomy 11:26-28 it says, See, I am setting before you today a blessing and a curse— 27 the blessing **if you obey** the commands of the Lord your God that I am giving you today; 28 the curse if you **disobey** the commands of the Lord your God and turn from the way that I command you today by following other gods, which you have not known."* Many claim to be obedient, but their disobedience is obvious in their lifestyles and actions. An alcoholic or addict is living under a curse, yet refuses to acknowledge that it has anything to do with being disobedient to God. Instead, the world has them convinced that they have a disease.

Fourth, we claim God's promises and blessings through the faith we've gained from our assurance and confidence in Christ, and His sacrifice for us on the Cross. *Hebrews 11:1, [Faith in Action] "Now **faith** is confidence in what we hope for and **assurance** about what we do not see." Ephesians 3:12, "In him and through **faith** in him we may approach God with freedom and **confidence**." Hebrews 4:16, "Let us then approach God's throne of grace with **confidence**, so that we may receive mercy and find grace to help us in our time of need." 1 John 5:14, "This is the **confidence** we have in approaching God: that if we ask anything according to his will, he hears us."*

Brothers and sisters in Christ, we're clearly living in the end times. Our churches have abandoned us by abandoning The Gospel Truth, just as Biblical prophecy has predicted. For the sake of fame, fortune, and power, they've exchanged God's Word for tolerance and acceptance to pagan worldly behavior and evil. They've neglected the lost, hurting souls trapped in addictions by counseling them with secular psycho-babble, rather than The Truth. Telling born again Christians that they're powerless, instead of taking the time to explain the Truth, (Acts 1:8) is blasphemy, yet thousands of churches today are guilty of this practice in their addiction recovery programs. The simplest answer for us to overcome this travesty, is to practice and follow the words in *Acts 17:11, "Now the Berean Jews were of more noble character than those in Thessalonica, for they received the message with great eagerness and examined the Scriptures every day to see if what Paul said was true."* If the Bereans knew in their days that they shouldn't trust a man of Paul's character, how much more vigilant should we be today? We must learn to trust only the Word of God, not mans! The only way to do that is to read our Bible daily. Our churches are filled with false teachers today who will lead us straight to hell! God has been warning us of this Truth since the Garden, and it's our responsibility to God to acknowledge and respond to His warnings.

    This should not come as a surprise to anyone. Today, we are exactly where God said we would be in the end times according to prophesy. The question is what are you going to do about it? The Truth is that Christ could return before you take another breath. That doesn't leave you with a lot of time to ponder your situation. Whether you're a Christian struggling with addictions, or not, do you want to spend whatever time is left trapped in bondage to addictions and other sin, or change the path you're on, and prepare for Eternity with God?

    As hopeless as addictions appear to be without Christ in a person's life, there is an answer, which is the same answer for all the issues regarding addictions, it's the same answer for all of mankind's shortcomings and failures; it's the message of the Gospel, and of Christ Crucified! The acceptance of this message in our lives brings Salvation, which brings freedom, which will lead us to take up our own cross, to the place where we can find peace and be **Saved and Sober!**

This book has been all about two very simple, but life changing Truths. The truth about satan's dark and evil world of sin and addictions, and the death and destruction it brings to the millions of people who refuse to listen to, and accept God's Truth. To those who refuse God's free offer of Salvation and Eternal life with Him. The other Truth shared on these pages has been of God's Love, Grace, and forgiveness, which produces light to expose the darkness and evil of sin and addictions. The purpose of this book was to reveal these two opposing Truths, through scripture as it applies to life in addiction recovery.

Addictions, (drunkenness, or sin), have been around since the fall of man in the garden. Drunkenness is mentioned first in Deuteronomy 29:19, and then immediately followed in verse 20, explaining the consequences of God's wrath and curses promised to the offenders. The consequences of all sin, including drunkenness, and the Blessings for those who choose to follow and obey God, have been the central focus of God's Word since the beginning of time. And man has been rejecting His Truth ever since then. One reason is that man hasn't been taught the Truth since the beginning, and certainly not in recent years in many Churches. False teachers have been around since the beginning of the church, and are prevalent throughout the world today.

It is a matter of eternal life or death that we understand in our own minds, God's Truth. Not from the minds and mouths of mere men, but from God's own Word spoken directly to us through the Holy Spirit and into our Hearts. Anything less than that can be detrimental to our Salvation and our recovery. As born again Christians in addiction recovery we shouldn't have a problem understanding this simple Truth. It's been the overall theme message throughout this book. While it might seem to have been repetitious, it's been my goal throughout this book to try to share and deliver this simple message from as many different viewpoints, and different vernaculars as possible so that a larger audience might understand why simply trusting God and surrendering your life to Him, in Faith, He will "set us free" indeed from the bondage of our addictions.

In closing, it is my prayer that everyone who has read this book has been following along with the scripture, allowing God to speak to their hearts, and reveal the Truth as it applies to their circumstances. I pray that any unsaved readers will feel the Holy Spirit leading them to Salvation and that *every* reader will recognize that only through God's infinite Love and Grace can we be **SAVED and SOBER!**

At the end of our journey of this life, we are all moving on to begin another. According to God, we all have the choice to decide where our next home will be. Either with Him, and with our loved ones, both past and present, who have accepted His invitation to join Him in Eternity, or with satan in hell. This message is clear and simple, not requiring a degree in rocket science, or theology to understand, nor is it conditional upon any cumbersome requirements, other than our full surrender to Him, confessing Him as our Lord and Savior, having the Faith of a mustard seed, and obeying His will for us, which has always been meant to benefit and Bless us. I pray that those who have taken the time to read this book, will have come to the conclusion that accepting God's free offer and gift of Salvation, will not only reward them with Eternal life with Him, but also provide a Blessed life here today with the opportunity to be

SAVED and SOBER!

If you've been patient enough to make it this far, congratulations. The Truth is hard for many to accept. Impossible for many others. For the few who can understand and appreciate it, you're clearly traveling a very narrow road, and heading for an even narrower gate at the end of the journey. (Matthew 7:14) If Salvation, Eternal Life, and addiction recovery are our number one priorities in life, we must choose to pick up our cross and follow Christ wherever He leads us. (Matthew 10:38) No matter how uncomfortable it may feel, or how many sacrifices might be required of us, we must answer His call in obedience. The longer we procrastinate in giving our "Utmost for His Highest," the longer we can expect to suffer the consequences. Addiction recovery will be but one of many rewards to follow our decision to give Him our utmost. That's not to say that there won't be obstacles along the journey, but that arriving at the final destination will far outweigh the bumps in the road, and the trials that God will place on our path to strengthen our character and Faith, so that when we arrive at the gate, we can hear the words that only a few will hear, "Well done my faithful servant!" (Matthew 25:23) I don't know about you, but those are the most important words I'm looking forward to ever hearing!

Finally my brothers and sisters in Christ, we're warned throughout God's Word to beware of false teachers and prophets, (2 Peter 2:1),...to beware of wolves in sheep's clothing, (Matthew 7:15, Acts 20:29). How do we do this you ask? There are false teachers everywhere, how do we protect ourselves and detect the deceitful ways of the enemy? We must put on the full armor of God, (Ephesians 6:11), and follow the words in Acts 17:11, we must be as the Bereans did, and examine, study, and meditate on God's Word daily, and compare it with whatever we're being taught. When in doubt, we need to pray and ask God Himself, for His divine inspiration, and if necessary, pray until our knees bleed! He **WILL** answer, in **HIS** timing! Trust Him! And be **SAVED and SOBER!**

Don't wait until the…

LAST CALL!

You can contact the author by visiting my website at w.w.w.addictioncrucifixionfellowship.com. From there you'll find a link to my Facebook page as well.

Made in the USA
San Bernardino, CA
07 September 2013